MAKING Y
HOME AND FU

MAKING YOUR OWN MONEY AT HOME AND FURTHER AFIELD!

With a few life hacks thrown in for good measure!

JANE CROSS

Published by Jane Cross Publishing

A CIP catalogue record for this book is available from the British Library.

ISBN 978-1-9996989-0-4

Book layout and cover design by Clare Brayshaw

Cover image © Andrii Yalanskyi | Dreamstime.com

Prepared and printed by:

York Publishing Services Ltd
64 Hallfield Road
Layerthorpe
York YO31 7ZQ

Tel: 01904 431213

Website: www.yps-publishing.co.uk

INTRODUCTION

This book is designed to help you earn money from the comfort of your own home (and beyond). There are times in our lives when for one reason or another we are unable to go out to work to earn our money. Working from home is a convenient way of earning money, you can work the hours that you want, when it suits you and do a wide range of things.

Maybe you just want to earn a bit of money on the side. I have listed an A to Z as a guide for you but I am sure you can even go further afield. Some of the jobs I have listed are not from home, but can still be done at your convenience. You may, for some of these need transport also. However, generally the majority of these can be done from your home. This book is developed to help you earn money at a time when it may be difficult for you to do so. So best of luck in finding your ideal job and earning an income.

No responsibility is taken for information that is no longer correct at time of printing. As this is a guide to help you earn money from home, you will need to do the up to date research for yourself. However, every attempt is made to give you the most up to date, accurate information possible. This book is designed to help you to help yourself!

However, you need to remember to calculate your expenses and costs as well as your tax and national insurance to be deducted from your earnings and this will determine your overall profits. You will be classed as self-employed and therefore will need to fill out a tax return for the year that you have worked. So remember to keep ALL of your receipts in a safe place and hold them for three years after that particular tax year you are registering for. You could be asked to produce them and any other information that refers to that year by HMRC.

Do not assume you can get away without paying the tax man, it is a legal requirement and they can and do impose prison sentences for those of whom evade paying HMRC (Her Majesty's Revenue and Customs). Not to mention the fines that are also imposed on you. So do it right from the start.

It is also wise to remember that they (HMRC) are also there to help you, so if you are in any difficulty in knowing what to do, then please give them a call. They want you to get it right, they are not there to catch you out. Getting it right first time saves a lot of aggravation in the long run and money that you may be fined if you get it wrong.

All businesses need to be registered at Companies House.

If you are claiming benefits, then find out how much you can earn (or how many hours you can work for) without it effecting you payments. You need to do this before you decide to go ahead with any of these activities or ventures.

Please read this book from start to finish to enable you to get the full benefit from it! That way you will then be fully aware of which venture is most suitable for you.

I hope you enjoy reading this as much as I have enjoyed writing it! I have included a few funny quips for you and some of my little life experiences for you to have a chuckle at!

A

Accountant

An accountant is, **a person whose job is to keep or inspect financial accounts.**

To become an accountant you would have to have a love of figures and a good grasp of them. If you manage to balance your budget from one month to the next then this is a good start to accountancy. You will need to study to become one. Luckily these days most studying can also be done from home and there are many ways for you to begin. If you are starting from the bottom and do not have a G.C.S.E grade of C or above in Maths (or English for that matter,) then the local government employment offices will put you in touch with your local college to apply for a free course. There are also Trade Unions who offer a lot of free courses for you including the English and Maths ones I have just mentioned above (these are available to you, if you are a member).

There are a range of different qualifications you can take to become an accountant.

Also please check your local employment office to see if you can get funding for this course or any other course you wish to take. There are also learning organisations on-line, such as **www.ofcourse.com** or **www.newskillsacademy.co.uk**, there are many more just use your search engine to find the names of them and look for one that suits you best. I find going to college to study in a classroom works for me.

You might also just want to do a short book-keeping course, which will allow you to work from home (as a Book-keeper) and I don't believe you need a degree in it to do it. Again use your search engine to check it out for yourself.

Advertising

Advertising is, **the activity or profession of producing advertisements for commercial products or services.**

If you own a car or a van then you can use it to advertise for other companies. **Carvetise** is a company that will pay you to advertise on your car. You can go to **www.carvetise.co.uk** for more information. **www.gocompare.com** also give you information on earning up to £1,000 a year by advertising on your car, this is a comparison website. You could also try **www.comparethemarket.com**, if you have more than one car, then you are laughing. Check other search engines for more price comparisons too. I have seen sides of houses advertising the business round the corner, so if you have a massive outside wall of your house then why not enquire about advertising on it.

Agricultural Fruit-Picker

A Fruit-Picker is, **a person or a tool that picks fruit.**

Check your local area for farmers markets and then ask them if they need workers. I find showing up at a Market and asking for work goes down quite well as they can see your personality and enthusiasm. Alternatively you can use a search engine to find out what is available in your area. You can also pick abroad if you are a student and fancy a summer in the sun. You may also get offered accommodation at a small cost to you. Some people are quite cynical about the pay grade, but others find it very therapeutic to switch off and leave the stress of the city behind them. Search **www.moneymagpie.com** for more information.

Allotment

An allotment is, **a plot of land rented by an individual for growing vegetables or flowers. Or the act of allotting something.**

Having an Allotment is a great way of saving money and making good use of your time, however, it is time consuming. You get out what you put in. It keeps you fit and healthy. You can get a list of allotments (in your area) from your local council. They charge a low annual fee which you pay up front. I find it a great way of sharing produce with your fellow plot holders (neighbours). Although if you have a big enough garden then this won't cost you a membership fee, you may not be able to swap your produce with your neighbour, but you might be able to swap your vegetables for your neighbour's homemade cakes (for example). You can only ask!!! If you enrol on some freebee sights, then you may bag yourself some free seeds. Check out **www.magicfreebiesuk.co.uk**

Alterations & Repairs

Alteration is **a change, usually a slight change, in the appearance, character, or structure of something.** Repair is **to restore (something damaged, faulty, or worn) to a good condition. The action of repairing something.**

Unless you are naturally gifted, or have had a previous profession in the altering and repairing side of retail clothing. Then do a short course at college or in your local town/village hall. Many people will make do and mend, rather than throwing away and replacing the item. This can be anything from elbow patches to replacement zips, or turning up a hem. There is an endless list of items, including furnishing repairs, curtain alterations and sofa covers are but just a few. Check local shops to see what they charge and this will give you a guide, remember you do have to buy the thread, zip, etc. Take this into account when charging. Make sure you buy the best quality, reputation is everything, it gives us more trade if it we have a good one. Also remember with fabric, you really should do these in a smoke and animal free area of your home. Smells do linger and non-smoking animal free customers will pick up on the odour instantly.

Amazon Dealer (Buying and Selling)

A dealer is, a **person who buys and sells goods.**

Amazon is worldwide, which means we can buy and sell worldwide. This can be done pretty much at our finger tips in any room of our home, or in the garden. Technology allows us to pretty much do anything. For example, maybe you are reading this book on **Amazon Kindle**, who knows. Maybe you are retired and are so passionate about your skill or trade that you want to share it with the world, then writing your own D.I.Y book could be your thing. I believe they get a small percentage of your sales. Checkout **Kindle Direct Sales**, this will give you all the info you need and it is their official site. You don't just have the book side of things, you can pretty much buy and sell anything. Check out the site and take a look for yourself, **www.amazon.co.uk**

Antique Dealer

An antique **is a collectable object such as a piece of furniture or work of art that has a high value because of its age and quality.** An antique dealer **works primarily in the buying and selling of antique items. They generally have a knowledge of antiques and what they are worth.**

Becoming an antique dealer may not be as hard as it seems. There are many antique books out there that show us what to look for and how much certain items are worth. Many of these books you will find in your local charity shop. (You will find some in the local library, however it is worth investing in the books, that way you will always have the information at hand when you need it.)

The down side of this is that you will need invest money in buying the said antique, before selling it to make the profit. Some antiques you may pick up from charity shops or boot markets and if the seller is unaware of the fact that these are valuable items, then you may be able to make a tidy profit.

Remember you get out what you put in, so study hard and the knowledge will be yours. Start small, invest little and make sure it is something you can sell on (and for a profit).

Apps

An App is, **an application, especially as downloaded by a user to a mobile device.**

There are short courses you can do and self-learning books you can buy to help you build an app. The question is knowing what app to design (what for), what design you want, (how to make the biggest impact to the consumer) and who you wish to sell the app to (if you don't want to keep it running for yourself).

For example if you build a gambling app, you could (as daft as it may seem) sell this to another gambling company or to an anti-gambling company. Let me explain, say for example you have a bingo app and another major bingo company wishes to buy it from you so as not to have you as the competition (they would still use the app if they so wished, but they would get the business, not have you take the business from them). Or anti-gambling campaigners or organisations may wish to buy it from you to prevent you from creating more gamblers (by not using the app). Or they may use the app and then use the profits to fund their organisation or charity (I am not saying that they will go down this route, but they have the possibility to do so).

The app you choose may have some meaning to you, or something you are passionate about. It may just be that it is something you have great knowledge about.
www.firebase.google.com/develop/app
www.scorchsoft.com (scorchsoft is Birmingham based)
www.square1.io/mobile-apps these are a few sites to have a look at.

Artist

An artist is, **a person who creates paintings or drawings as a profession or hobby.**

If you want to be an artist then you can do a course, either at your local college or on-line through a viable company. There are also many books on how to be an artist. The decision would be what to learn, painting, drawing, or you can even diverse into sculpture or pottery, and the possibilities are endless. Whatever (or whoever) inspires you.

There are also tutorials on line to help you and you can do weekend courses in painting and pottery, possibly even sculpture and drawing. Whatever you decide will undoubtedly earn you money if you aim to sell it to the right buyer (ones that pay you the most money for your work).

Art galleries are a good way of getting your work seen and seen by the right people at the right time. Just make sure you have enough stuff to exhibit. You would also need to get advice from the gallery you wish to use. But first you need to study and get to grips with being an artist, this isn't done overnight.

Avon Caller

To be an Avon Rep then go to **www.rep-uk.com** this site will give you access to become a seller.

Or go to **www.avon.uk.com** once on the site, you can scroll down to the bottom of the home page and click on become a rep. If there is no other seller in your area then you could cash in on quite a lot. But this is a job that will require a lot of effort in the beginning. You would have to seek out clients, deliver booklets, place orders, deliver products, collect the money and keep up your selling techniques from one month to the next.

Some seasons you may earn more than others, such as Christmas, Valentine's Day, Mother's Day and Easter, there may be a hard slog to sell at other times of the year.

However if you know how to sell ice to Eskimo's then you are a winner. You can also hold parties round customer's houses to generate more clients and this could be done when you have a seasonal slump.

B

Bank Account Transfer

I recently changed my bank account (one I have had for many years, so believe me when I say it was one of the most difficult decisions in my life) to one which offered to pay me £150 for transferring and allowed me to save £250 a month at 5% interest.

My previous account reduced its rate to 2% and only allowed me to save £200 a month. I was still offered the same overdraft as I had with my old account. It just meant that I gained a higher interest rate from my savings and cash for switching. It was a win, win situation, a no brainer really. But it made me feel disloyal, however, if my bank could offer me this then why couldn't the one I had been loyal to for over a decade?!

Some account switching offer less than mine, but if you go to **www.moneysavingexpert.com** you can find out more information on it. You need to do your research to find out what is best for you.

Basket Maker

A basket maker is, **a person who makes baskets.**

There are many adult courses you can do at your local college, some libraries do group meetings, local town or village halls. There are self-teach books as well that can help you do most things. I am sure Basket Making is included. If you cannot afford a course or buy a book and don't have internet access, the use your local library's resources. Such as half an hour a day free internet use, rent out books, (make sure you bring them back on time, otherwise you will be fined,) reference books can be used in the library to study.

You would just need to pay for your materials. This can be quite therapeutic and can be done in the comfort of your own home or outside in your garden (if you have one).

I have (whilst driving through Europe,) seen basket makers sitting outside their front door on a chair weaving away. You need to source out a buyer for them though and make sure it is worth your while. Christmas hampers, Picnic baskets, Easter baskets, Valentines baskets and Halloween are but a few ideas.

Beautician

A beautician is, **a person whose job is to give people beauty treatment.**

Being a beautician can be a little costly with all your creams and treatments, however the rewards can be a lot greater than your costs. You can use your own creams to practice with on friends (everyone loves a free facial). There are many courses online you can do as well as online tutorials and blogs to show you great techniques.

Once you get your confidence up and your qualifications then you can start your own business. You can work from home (if you have a spare room, then that could work as a treatment room). You could even be a mobile beautician, freelance for hotels which offer spa treatments for their guests. Do pre-wedding packages, special birthday treatments or even mother's day packages. You may find doing a short business course beneficial.

The possibilities are endless.

Become a Blogger

A Blogger is, **a person who regularly writes for a blog. A blog is a regularly updated website or web page, typically run by an individual or small group that is written in an informal or conversational style.**

A lot of money can be made from Blogging, it depends on what your blog is about, how popular it is (in other words are people interested in it). I do believe (but you need to check it out for yourself,) that it all depends how many hits you have (or followers), to how much money you can earn.

Again there are self-help books that teach you how to blog. **www.simplesite.com** shows you how to create a blog for free, so do **www.emyspot.com**. There are many teach yourself books you can purchase, so what are you waiting for?!

Become a Lord or Lady

A Lord is, **a man of noble rank or high office, a nobleman. Confer the title of Lord upon**. A Lady is, **a polite or formal way of referring to a woman. A woman of good social position.**

www.highlandtitles.com is the place to search, you buy a small plot of land (approximately one square foot) for about £30 which gives you the right to the title. If you get this put onto your passport (as apparently, you are allowed to use the title), then drivers licence, you can then receive preferential treatment. You may receive upgrades on flights, upgrade of hotel rooms, upgrade of car hire, better tables in restaurants and just be treated better in general.

You will however have to act the part, a Lord or Lady isn't likely to have an ASBO (Anti-Social Behaviour Order, which (I believe) is now referred to as Community Protection Notice CPN, or Criminal Behaviour Order CBO) against them, so please don't act like you have. I don't mean act upper class, just be polite and well-mannered, it may open up a few doors for you.

Once when I was about to board a flight I was ushered to the speedy boarding side and that was just because I was holding a copy of the financial pages of a well-known newspaper in my hand. I do (occasionally) read the paper and when this happened, it didn't take me long to figure out why. Their theory (I believe) was that if I bought this newspaper, then I was likely to have a portfolio in either shares or property, so I was relatively a well to do person.

Although it'd not always good to declare you are a Lord or Lady, for example when you need the builders in, they may bump up your bill accordingly. So use the title when and where you can benefit from it, after all that is my purpose for including this in the book.

Beekeeper

A beekeeper is, **a person who owns and breeds bees, especially for their honey.**

If you have a large garden (and I do mean large) or some land, such as a small holding, then in your spare time you could be a bee keeper. Ideally you would have a garden full of flowers (this is great for bees, some flowers are better for bees than others so as always do your research). Companies can come in and place a bee hive for you and then come and empty the honey. Depending on how many hives you have and how much honey it makes, will determine what you get paid (a jar of honey, or some money!). You are also doing your bit to keep our bees alive. **www.localhoneyman.co.uk** is just one site you can check out. Search engine it to find more sites available to you in your area.

Be on a show

So you can check this out in your search engine, there are so many shows to be on. Ones that can win you money and prizes, others that can find your dream home, some here and some overseas depending on where you want to live. It's not from home but if you have time on your hands then this (quiz shows) is a great way of getting some money in your pocket. Quiz shows may require you to read up on a few topics, but you have time so that's no bother. You may already be someone who reads a lot. So if you are not camera shy then give it a go!! Check out **itv.com/beontv** why not try the shows that gives money to the runners up as well.

I am watching a quiz show as I write this.

Betterware Salesperson

A salesperson is, **salesman or saleswoman (used as a neutral alternative).**

www.betterware.co.uk has the same principles as the **Avon** caller, (go to the A section in this book,) it is door to door selling, with booklets, holding parties and delivering the goods. If you can do one, then you can do the other.

Bicycle Restore

A restorer is, **a person who repairs or renovates a building, work of art etc. So as to return it to its original condition.**

Have you ever been to an auction and seen a load of bicycles being bought by the same person?! Then this maybe why. Buying an old bike for next to nothing, doing it up and selling it for less than the price of a new one (especially near Christmas time) is a business for some people.

If you like restoring then even better, it is rewarding financially and mentally, as well as being quite therapeutic. You will need to get info on how to fix (and do maintenance on) bikes as a minimum or buy a book on bike restoration, you can even do a short course in bike maintenance, unless you already know how to do it and if you do, then what is keeping you?!

There will be a small outlay of buying the bike, the cost of material. (Some of which you can reuse on the next project, such as spanners. You may need to buy spray paint and sand paper, and more, remember to buy the best quality it will make all the difference in the final appearance of the bike.)

Boot market Stallholder

A stallholder is, **a person owning or running a stall at a market.**

If you are a bit of a hoarder, I don't mean with newspapers from floor to ceiling in your home. Just a bit like me, a person who thinks that the sandwich toaster on sale for less than £10 was a bargain and then buys it and ends up storing it in the garage for the next 3 years. Then why not do a boot market for a clear out and get some money in your pocket.

I personally love getting up at the crack of dawn to go set up a stall and sell my stuff. You generally make the most money in the first couple of hours. Most dealers are the first to check out your goods. Charge a little more than you want and be prepared to be haggled down.

You will need a table or a blanket to put your stuff on. If you intend to do one each week, then maybe you should invest in a clothes rail. You will be charged a small fee for your pitch, but if you have lots of stuff, then it will be worth it. You will need a bag full of change too.

Boot markets are one way to sell any craft stuff you have made or any homeware you have such as cushions, blankets, rugs, old dinner sets, etc. That's the best thing about having a go, you can sell almost anything you have or make and your overheads are relatively low. Okay so you won't make a fortune per item, but you may well sell a lot of your stock, which will generate a nice day's earner. It will give you a good clear out of your home, garage or shed.

If you do this regularly than you can re-invest it in more stock (make sure the new stock is profitable, if it costs me £1 to buy I want to make sure I get £2 when I sell it, or £1.50 at least).

British Sign Language Teacher/Translator

A teacher is, **a person who teaches, especially in a school.**

A translator is, **a person who translates from one language to another, especially as a profession.**

There is a lot of campaigning to get Sign Language put into the school curriculum. I personally feel that this is a fantastic idea. If children were taught this at a young age then any deaf child can go into mainstream schools where they can mix with their friends, their next door neighbours, the other kids on the street. I would love to see it nationally, there is nothing greater than knowledge and the art of communication is precious and priceless. Inclusion or exclusion, I rest my case.

I have personally done the Basic 1 British Sign Language Course and even though it was 20 years ago, I still know some signs and the whole of the alphabet, however even I need a refresher. There is a Basic 1 and then you go onto do the Level 2 course.

The IBSL **(Institute of British Sign Language)** will determine whether you can teach or not, they will also advise you if you need a Master's degree or not. I believe that you will need something on this level to Interpret.

If you have a child that is deaf, then the Basic 1 and Basic 2 will become invaluable to you. They do cost money, however my employer at the time paid half of mine which was a massive help. Obviously it depends on your employer and where you work to determine whether or not they will help fund the course. Working with the public, children or people who sign will help with your request for funding, but be prepared for a 'sorry but there is no money in the kitty' reply.

Make sure when requesting it, that you put it in writing and choose your words carefully. I have found that it is how you put something that determines whether you get it or not.

Makaton is also a form of sign language, which (I believe) uses the main signs in a sentence, rather than signing every word. You still know what they are saying, it's a bit like broken English. Use your search engine to download free sign posters which can help you learn how to do it.

C

Cake Maker

A cake maker is, **a food preparation worker who makes cakes.**

I am sure I don't need to tell you the difference between the visual impacts of having a supermarket bought cake, compared to one that has been specifically created for you. There is so much more to baking cakes than baking, these days you really need to be into sculpture. So baking cakes is the start of it, if you can follow a recipe then your half way there. There are so many books, on-line tutorials, weekend courses for you to choose from to learn how to create the visual masterpiece you are after.

To practice on sculpture then make up some pastry and use that to work with. This is a great product to use. You don't want to jump straight in and use icing as it will harden up quickly which is not practical if you are trying to practice with it. From making figurines to flower petals. Use the icing once you feel you have mastered it.

Creative masterpieces are paid well for and word of mouth goes far and wide, especially if you get it right for your client. I don't just mean birthday cakes either, tier wedding cakes can earn you a nice bit of cash. Remember to keep a portfolio of all your works of art, clients won't take your word for it, they need to see what you do and quite rightly so. Would you just assume that someone can make your wedding cake, without checking before, because it can ruin your special day if it's not right?!!

The best tip I can give you is do not cut corners with costs, buy the best ingredients, especially in your flour and butter. Remember the saying 'the proof is in the pudding'. Also the best tools you can buy, you don't want to be replacing them in a hurry, you want them to last you a good few years!

Always remember to list all ingredients and allergens!

Last but not least, always listen to what your client wants, don't try and recreate a masterpiece of your own desire, if that wasn't what they asked you for!

Carer

A carer is, **a family member or paid helper who regularly looks after a child or sick, elderly, or disabled person.**

Becoming a carer is more of a vocation, or calling if you like. It's not necessarily a 9 til 5 job, depending if you are a live-in carer or a day or night shift worker. You may already be caring for a family member. If you are then you need to contact your local benefits office to see what carer's allowance you can claim, especially if it is taking you away from earning a wage outside your home. If you are a full-time carer, then have a look at some of the other jobs in this book that you could do at home in some of your free time, maybe whilst the person you are caring for is resting or sleeping. It will still let you work from home caring, but give you a paid hobby also, if you like. Obviously choose one that you can do when you want to, like quilt making, something creative. I wouldn't advise gaming as you are supposed to be caring for someone. Those that do gaming do it for hours on end and you can't leave your patient for such a long time without checking on them.

Obviously this doesn't apply to you if you are caring for a family member, but to work in the caring profession you would need to have gone through a police check. You would also need to have done some basic training on how to care for your patient. If you have previously cared for a family member then this would have been useful to you when looking for work. Once you have the qualifications, the police check and registered yourself, then you can look for work, either locally in your neighbourhood or further afield (if you are thinking of travelling further you would need your own transport, or have access to it).

On the plus side you would not need a high lay out of cost, yes if you need training then that will cost you, but that will be a one off payment, then a uniform, if it is not supplied. Generally though if you are working in your local neighbourhood, then you won't even need a car, you could possibly walk, cycle or if necessary get a bus.

If you are a child carer, looking after your parent or grandparent then try to find some 'Me time'. What you do is an amazing thing and you should be very proud of yourself. However, there is help available for you which can give you time out, with your friends, so you can enjoy yourself without feeling guilty, knowing that the person you are caring for is being looked after.

Car Maintenance

Maintenance is, **the process of preserving a condition or situation or the state of being preserved.**

Doing a car maintenance course at your local college will save you a lot of money in car servicing and can help preventing a costly M.O.T failure. I also believe that we should all have a basic knowledge of our vehicle, I personally do not want my car to break down and without a basic understanding of car maintenance I would be stumped! This is not just for the men in our world, women could save a fair few pounds by just having a bit of knowledge. Only last week I drove to my local slimmer's group and as I parked the car, the Engine Failure light came on. I quickly weighed in and drove straight back home. I was terrified that I wouldn't make it back. Thankfully I did make it, however it brought home to me how uneducated I am in car maintenance. I also do not want to have to rely on my husband knowing more than me (he isn't that knowledgeable when it comes to cars, but he has more knowledge that I do).

I also remember travelling with my dad (in his little van) when I was a youngster (about 10 years old). We were driving through Brixton when it broke down. I had to get out and push, while my dad steered it. Can you imagine it, a little chubby kid (I was), pushing a van through the town of Brixton and yes within minutes the residents were all on their door steps pissing themselves laughing. I am crying with laughter as I write this, it was a comical situation. My dad wasn't exactly thin either, pushing that van was a hard task.

There was another time when my dad had a mini bus type van, (it was an orange thing), I was with him when the wheel fell off, literally. It was so corroded, we were driving in Maidstone when suddenly we tilted. My mother was not impressed with him, to say the least. He wasn't best pleased either, he had to get us a taxi to get us back home, it was a good few miles away and cost him a fair few quid.

My point is that you can see the importance of looking after your vehicle and regular car maintenance and servicing can prevent such incidents and accidents. Joking aside losing a wheel off your vehicle in mid transit (so to speak) could be very dangerous, we were very lucky.

Motorcycle maintenance is also worth doing if that is your chosen vehicle. I once broke down on mine right in the centre of town, I couldn't even change the gears to move it. It wasn't going to budge. There was a lot of car horns tooting at me at the time, I can never understand why people choose to let you know that you are in their way, when clearly you know that you are! Having a whole load of cars pushing on their horns as they drive past you is not going to get your bike to do what you want any quicker, their only accomplishment is to make you feel even more embarrassed and stressed at the situation. Just saying!!

Cashback

Cashback is, **a form of incentive offered to buyers of certain products whereby they receive a cash refund after making their purchase.**

There are many companies and banks for that matter that give you cash back. It is well worth checking them out. I try to go through cashback sites when booking on line, especially holidays. It's not a massive amount you get back, however if you add the amounts up it comes to a few quid. I received almost £50 back from my package holiday which paid for a meal out once we arrived there. So there really is such a thing as a free lunch! Check out **www.topcashback.co.uk** for an idea of what you can claim back, you will have to follow the links on the site to go to the particular businesses that you want to buy from. It is certainly worth the saving. If all your family members used a cashback site, then you as a family could end up with a few pounds in your pocket which could be used on a well-deserved break or to fund a course or two!!

Also check out **www.quidco.com** for cashback.

Casting Extra

A casting extra is, **a person who is still considered a background performer, but is potentially recognizable in the final product.**

When film makers need extras they generally advertise the fact in the local newspaper of the town they are filming in. There's a website called **www.starnow.co.uk/Extras** this will set you in the right direction, get yourself well known in the industry then well, who knows what can happen and where it can lead you to. There is a small membership fee on this website, (however they do help you build a portfolio too) so check out a few search engines for yourself. Casting extras generally get paid depending on the project itself. Usually it is from £50 to £150 per day. Okay so you won't get work for a whole week for 48 weeks of the year, but this book is designed to help you earn money without the fulltime job label attached to it, to help you work for yourself and do what you would love to do and where possible, to do it from home.

Catering

Catering is, **the provision of food and drink at a social event or other gathering.**

Catering can come in all shapes and sizes, you can cater for a cold lunch consisting of sandwiches, scotch eggs and pastries. Or you can do a buffet, or you can cater for a wedding. What you will need though is access to a kitchen (preferably at the venue).

Using your own home is okay if you are baking cakes to sell (at least I think it is, you may need to check this out for yourself though), but anything else would require a more in-depth investigation in to whether or not you would need a separate kitchen, with food hygiene standards checked by the food hygiene standards agency.

This agency would also give you advice on what you can and cannot do, they are not (contrary to popular belief) there just to pick up on the bad things. You will need to get yourself a food hygiene certificate, this doesn't cost much, ask the agency what you need to do and how to get it done. Remember, they are not your enemy, they want you to do well.

The outlay for this would be, platters, crockery, cutlery, cups and saucers, glassware, table cloths, utensils (such as tongs) the list can be extensive. Not excluding the food stuff, you need to remember some clients won't pay it all up front so you may have to wait until after the event.

Never buy poor quality food to cut corners, your reputation will precede you, so make sure it is a good one. Again, take photos, get yourself a portfolio to be proud of, remember the smaller functions too. Sometimes it is better to have lots of little ones rather than a few large ones. The larger ones will require you to employ staff to help you serve and they will need to be paid by you, not wait for you to be paid.

Always remember to list the ingredients and allergens. You also need to know how to cook and make sure you don't cause any food poisoning to anyone.

Don't forget to register your company, remember the tax man (HMRC) and any insurances you may need.

Cattery

A cattery is, **a boarding or breeding establishment for cats.**

Okay you seriously need to be a cat lover for this. Or at least love animals in general. The idea of this is not to build an outhouse for it, but if you have one then all the better. You may need to research cats behaviours so you don't end up with a massive cat fight in your living room. But generally your home can be turned into a cattery if you so wish. I have a neighbour who refers to herself as 'the cat lady' self-explanatory really. Okay, so you can look after cats while their owners are on holiday and your expense would only be the food, cat litter and your time. Although you cannot squeeze 20 cat into a one bedroom flat, no matter how big the room is, it is not practical. So do not overstretch yourself.

Preferably have a garden with a cat flap, but secure the area surrounding you, as some of these cats won't be familiar with your neighbourhood. Always check with their owner that they can be let out. Also check any eating preferences or habits these felines may have (it may sound funny, but animals can have strange habits, best to find out what they are). Make sure you check to see if you need to have liability insurance for this one.

Dog walkers charge around £20 a day to walk your dog. To be a dog sitter I think that is about £25 a day, but some may charge more and some slightly less, but on average it's about £25, cats however don't need walking so it may vary a little. You may need to research it and then negotiate a price agreeable by you and the owner(s).

Chess Champion/Tournament

A champion is, **a person who has surpassed all rivals in a sporting contest or other competition.**

A tournament is, **a series of contests between competitors, competing for an overall prize.**

First you need to know how to play chess. Once you have mastered that then you need to practice with an opponent, either an electric chess set which plays against you or someone to play against. You have to work at getting it right and to have a set time to make your move, once you have mastered this you can start going to competitions/tournaments. Search the **FIDE** the World Chess Federation handbook, which offers guidelines and regulation for conducting such tournaments, this will give you an understanding of what to expect. Then search for tournaments locally and then nationally.

There are three prizes £500, £1000 and £1500 for players who didn't win a higher regular/rating prize in the Open Section of the tournament. This information may change over time, so check out for yourself more up to date information through your search engine.

The Isle of Man International Chess Masters (check out **www.iominternationalchess.com**) prizes are at £1,500 for the 11th place, going up to £50,000 for the first prize. If players have the same score and win first prize then they may have to share it, so be the best.

For the Ladies, 7th place is £500 and first place is £7,000. Again, this may change over time, so do your research.

This is one of my favourite ways of making money from your own home. Okay so you do have to venture out to win the major tournaments, but if you are stuck at home then you have a lot of hours to practice to make perfect your ability to win. With prize funds like this, the win is big! Plan ahead, when you have the date for the tournament, make your travel plans, if you cannot afford a hotel or B&B then hire a caravan or even go with a tent, if you can physically put it up and are physically fit enough to sleep on the ground.

If you can afford a hotel then stay in one, you don't need the added stress of sleeping on a cold ground if you don't have to.

If you have a disability then make sure you are accommodated for in the hotel and at the tournament. Don't allow a physical disability to hold you back, all you need for chess is your mental ability to play it and play it well. (Obviously you would need to move the chess pieces, but if you can play chess then you are already doing it, aren't you!?)

If like me you do not know how to play chess, then go to **www.wikihow.com** this website will give you a step by step guide of how to play.

Chicken Egg Farmer

A farmer is, **a person who owns or manages a farm.**

As in farming chickens for eggs, so you will need Hen's, a chicken run and egg boxes (ideally). I have in the past had a plot on an allotment and a fellow plotter had a few chickens and I did envy them somewhat. I have also seen a neighbour with ducks in their garden quite a few of them and they were selling the eggs from the front porch. So if you're starting off then buy a chicken run with two chickens, a hen and a rooster (cockerel). I think two hens to one rooster will give you a few eggs and not too much noise for your neighbours. I would start with one of each though, that may be enough and if you don't need more eggs, then stick with that amount.

You may not make enough to sell but making enough to eat will do, any extra then give them to your neighbour or swap them with them for something they have, like some homemade cake or bread.

Roosters can make an early morning noise, if yours does, then maybe give your nearest neighbour(s) a couple of eggs a week to smooth it over. No rooster, no eggs, they will soon get used to the noise, or having the eggs! Obviously half a dozen eggs would be better to give them, but just see what you can afford to give out first. There is no point only having enough eggs to feed your neighbours and nothing for yourself, you might as well not bother at all.

So the cost side of things is buying two chickens, chicken run and chicken feed. If you have a small holding then you could make a business out of this, but that is a different matter entirely.

You need to check laws and regulations before you start, make sure you have a vet in place (in case of such things like chicken flu, for instance) and your cost for egg boxes. Regulations will let you know what you need.

If you are not doing this as a business and only have a couple of hens you still need to know about chicken and bird flu, as you may need to keep the chickens inside for a period of time until the flu is cleared up. Remember to do all your research and checks first before deciding to invest in buying them.

Chiropodist

A chiropodist is, **a person who treats feet and their ailments.**

For me chiropody is something I wouldn't like to do as a profession, however, if I had to I would. But seriously some feet can be quite gross and cheesy, so rather you than me. However, this is quite a lucrative profession and as we are all about making money, here it is.

So, you need to be qualified and registered, which you need a degree which can take 3 years (or more), which is full time so you won't be able to work full-time. This is what you need to do to get there, once you have this degree you can work from home.

The going rate for a visit from your chiropodist at the moment is about £30 (that's what I have just paid) and it is for less than an hour's work on your feet, but more than half an hour. So if you are a mobile chiropodist you have to take in account your travel time, fuel cost, wear and tear of your vehicle, tax and national insurance, creams and tools etc. So take that away from your £30 and you could probably be clearing £15. Which is still a good earner, to work when and where you want. Have as much time off as you want and work around any children's school holidays if you need to.

£15 an hour, if you average 6 hours a day for 5 days a week, then you could clear £450 a week for a 30 hour week. Over a month that could be £1800 after costs and stoppages, such as tax and National Insurance, (this is a rough estimate, you need to contact the tax man for a better, more accurate guide).

If you have a spare room in your home you could work your business from there and not have travel costs at all and your working time can be cut down quite considerably. You could also do all your chores in between clients and still work around the school run and holidays. If you are a single parent this would be ideal, your children wouldn't even realise you worked because you would always be there. This job isn't just for women!! So please don't be put off by the stereotyping of it. Men can also have a lucrative career in chiropody.

Chocolate Maker

A chocolate maker is, **a person who makes chocolate.**

www.wikihow.com shows you what ingredients you need and a step by step guide on how to make chocolate, there are other search engines to use and books you can buy as well as on-line tutorials. A friend of mine made some for Christmas and they were lovely. You will need the cost of the ingredients, the packaging and how long it takes to make should be taken into consideration. As always the proof is in the pudding, so make sure they taste good, give out samples after dinner or to work colleagues, ask for an honest opinion, or just check out their face, you should normally tell if they like it or not. If they go for another one then clearly they do. Do this in the autumn and then you can make batches for Christmas to either sell at a Christmas Fayre or give as gifts.

Check out the local groups or competitions for the best chocolate cake for example, you could incorporate the two together. Competitions that you can win a cash prize are ones to look out for, or to win a course with a top Chef, or even get yourself to apply to go on a baking competition on the telly, there are lots to choose from, there is so much potential from something so small and quite easy to do.

Remember to do your food hygiene course (it doesn't cost much) and check out from the food standards agency before you sell your chocolate. You don't have to worry about it as much if you are doing competitions or giving it to friends, but it's still worth a call to them to double check. Remember researching anything you want to do is paramount in the success of it and stops us getting into any bother with the relevant authorities.

The Women's Institute do competitions for cakes, jam's, chutneys and so on. You need to search it, there is normally an annual one in the summer (I believe), check it out and check out the prizes too. I don't believe it is (the fetes) just for women either.

Always list your ingredients and allergens, you wouldn't want a reputation for causing an allergic reaction, or heaven forbid a fatality. So do it right first time!

Cinema Tickets

I have done this my-self! I bought travel insurance for a couple of days in order to get the 2 for 1 cinema tickets. It was worth it, I also found that when I needed any travel insurance I went to this particular website to get it. If you like going to the pictures each week then this could save you quite a few quid which could end up a nice sum over a year. I believe you can only use them on a Tuesday or a Wednesday, you would also need to check which cinemas are participating in the offer. Our local cinema does, you would need to check out your one. So next time you go to a comparison website then check out the benefits you can receive from them. **www.comparethemarket.com .**

Cleaner

A cleaner is, **a person employed to clean the interior of a building.**

You can earn anything from £10 to £20 an hour depending on your location. Your good reputation will gain you more work and before long you will have to either employ someone to help you or stop taking on new clients.

You will need transport, because you will need to take all your cleaning equipment with you including your vacuum cleaner. When working out your costs remember, cleaning cloths, dusters, cleaning fluids, fuel, wear and tear of you vehicle, etc. Also remember when paying tax and National Insurance to keep all your receipts of outgoings, including your mobile phone, the cost of a laptop to do your accounts (if you have bought one to do them). Also the cost of the vacuum cleaner.

Just remember though, some people need cleaners because their house is in dire need of a clean and the first visit may well be the worst visit. Others may just need a basic clean and tidy. Cleaning is very rewarding though, as you can step back and feel proud of what you have done.

Clothes Seller

A clothes seller is, **a person who sells clothes.**

There are some charitable places that buy your unwanted clothes, they pay by the kilo and have to be clean and in a good condition for them to buy from you.

You can also sell anything on-line and at boot markets.

You won't make mega bucks, but you will be able to have a good clear out and get some cash back at the same time.

However, if you have a scheme where you are, that may need some items for the homeless and you don't really need the fiver you might get for it, then maybe you can donate it to them. Be it a jacket, blanket or an old pair of boots that are still in a good condition. Maybe even an old food flask, hat, scarf or gloves! It's just a thought!

Computer Programmer/Engineer

A programmer is, **a person who writes computer programs. An engineer is, a person who designs, builds, or maintains engines, machines or structures.**

I worked for a company which whilst I was on the computer it had a funny moment and wouldn't do something that I wanted it to do. So I called our I.T. department and was instructed what to do after the I.T. guy had already done it. He wanted me to do the other computer as well and so I did the same thing without him telling me what to do. He was watching what my computer was doing from where he was (well watching what I was doing to the computer.) When I had finished he said how impressed he was, to be honest I was quite chuffed too. He was probably paid a salary for what he was doing and I was paid a mere wage. Never the less, it felt good to do it. There are so many I.T. courses out there that are accessible from the comfort of your own home. You need a computer and internet access. The cost will be of the course and if you do have a job, then most courses can be done in your own time at your own pace.

The average salary for a qualified I.T. person is £25,000 this went up in March 2019 by 9%, according to **totaljobs.com**, so if you think you would fancy a job in I.T. then check out the on-line courses which are available for you.

Couponing

Many years ago you could obtain coupons from local free papers and magazines. These days you need to look further, you need to search engine vouchers, and money off codes and so on. I have managed to get some from sites such as

www.supersavvyme.co.uk you do need to be clever about it though. If you have a £1 off voucher for a product, then (if the date is still valid for a few months) wait until the product is on a special offer for a pound. I have done this with fresh soups, in the chillers of the supermarket and this I have done many a time. Which makes it a free meal. So there is such a thing as a free lunch. You might want to invest in a printer if you are getting your vouchers on-line. Or use your local library, they really don't charge much per page, just a few pence. You get half an hour free use on their computers a day, so organise yourself so as to get the most out of your half hour. You can pay for more time (I believe), but why would you want to???

I have watched many programmes about couponing overseas and these people are seriously clued up on what they do and how to get their whole shop for nothing. It is a profession, you need to be well organised and spend a lot of time working out your shop and coupons before you go. Including spending hours cutting the coupons up, checking out what offers are on and what is your maximum allowance. Check it out on-line and watch a couple of programmes on it, it might give you the inspiration you need.

Craft Maker

A craft is, **an activity involving skill in making things by hand.**

Craft making can be making absolutely anything you want from patchwork quilts to napkin holders. And these are the things you can make throughout the year and have it all ready to sell at a Christmas Fayre in the autumn. Patchwork quilts can be bought for over £100 in certain department stores, so if you know of any fancy quirky vintage shops then try to sell it to them for £60 or do a sale or return basis. I doubt it will be returned to you, however it will mean that they will pay you when they sell it. But it beats getting £10 from a market stall (if you're lucky). The costs will be so much per week, to buy the patches, cotton etc. So you're out lay shouldn't be all at once and you will need to keep the items until you sell them. Which could be a few months. Although vintage shops would probably take some of your items as soon as you have made them, but be prepared to wait until nearer Christmas for them to sell them for you. You will need transport to go round and deliver them to whomever you are selling them to, but you could probably rent a car for a couple of days if you don't have one and get it all done in those two days. Or rope in a friend with a car to help you for a day. Correspond with your client by phone, send pictures via email and then make the deal so that when you deliver you know that they already want it, so there is no time lost. This is for someone with a lot of time on their hands, it can be very therapeutic work, so give it a go, start off small and see how you get on. There are untold amounts of craft books available, tutorials that show you how to make things, the possibilities are endless.

Check out your local village hall for classes in quilt making and any other craft workshops they may have on offer.

Crochet knitter

Crochet is, **a handicraft in which yarn is made up into a textured fabric by means of a hooked needle.**

A knitter is, **a person who makes garments (or fabrics) by intertwining yarn or thread.**

As before with craft making, crochet is craftwork, but in its own right, it has so many creative possibilities on its own. There are weekly magazines (which have a step by step guide) for you to buy as well as books, on-line tutorials and even crochet classes in some stores that sell wool and patterns, as well as adult evening classes to teach you techniques.

Crochet blankets are all the rage, as well as cardigans, doilies, dresses, hats, neck scarves, foot stalls, rugs, recycled carrier bags, the list goes on. If you have a lot of old tee-shirts, then if you cut strips off of them, then knot them to each other making a long string of strip. You can then crochet this into a large rug for your bathroom or sell it. Use the colours that suit your décor, or use bright multicolours to sell or neutral colours as people have different tastes or do both that way you have a chance to sell two. Try to find a vintage shabby chic shop to sell it for you, you will earn more money than selling it at a boot market.

The outlay can be old clothes you want to throw out, which will cost you nothing and upcycling them is a great way to get something out of the cost of nothing.

For clothing you need to buy whatever wool or fabric you want to use, it is always better to buy quality stuff, that way you should be able to get more money when you sell it and pick who you want to sell the item to, wisely. If you sell it to a boutique style shop then you are likely to get more than if you sell it on-line through a selling forum.

Don't forget to take photos, build a portfolio to be proud of, with this you can walk into a boutique show them your photos, discuss which they would like, go off and make it, then you are not wasting their time or yours.

Any materials you do need to buy though, you need to check that after outgoings, including tax and national insurance that you are going to have a sizeable profit at the end of it, otherwise it's not worth it. Unless you are upcycling, then you are already on a profit.

D

Dart Player

I have recently watched a few darts tournaments on the telly and there is no reason why I shouldn't include this as a way of earning money. Yes, you will have to eventually venture out, the same as if you were going to a chess tournament. However all you need to practice with is a dart board and a set of darts. Once you have mastered it, then you need to go out and get involved in playing in pubs or tournaments. Whichever way you choose is up to you. But the idea will be to eventually win money at tournaments. This is not just for men, or older or younger people. This should be for everyone at every age, (as long as there is no age restriction), so check out the requirements for yourself. I recently watched a young lady play in a tournament full of men, she was the only female. The crowd absolutely loved her, I believe she reached the semi-final. Even her opponent praised her.

Dog Sitter

I remember walking a friend's dog, using the same park that she used, on this visit I was asked by a member of the public (a friend of my friend) if I dog sit too. I immediately said "No!" in my defence, she had a Rottweiler. Joking a side, dog sitting is the new house sitting with a dog thrown in for good measure. So you get to use someone else's electric, hot water, heating and gas and not your own. However, you have to walk the dog (all be it large or small), twice a day. You also need to feed it, bath and groom it too. As I had previously said it's about £25 a day to dog sit, which isn't bad if you are not a worker, because otherwise you may have to take a week's holiday to do it, which is such a false economy. I was once asked to do just that, to take a week's holiday to look after someone's dogs for a week. Obviously I said no! I was offered £25 a day to do it, as that apparently is the going rate. I only get 22 days holiday a year I intend to use them for its purpose of a holiday! They were not amused, but I stood my ground and told them that even if I couldn't afford a holiday, I preferred to spend my free time in my home, not theirs! Families Eh!

If you are a student or you are working from home and you can still do that in someone else's house and get paid for it, then dog sitting is for you!

Not to be confused with dogging!

Dog Walker

Dog walkers get a fair wage, but more importantly you get exercise. Ever seen someone walking four or five dogs at a time, the likelihood is that they are a dog walker. And I bet they were not overweight. So if you need to walk more, then become a dog walker, lose weight and get paid for it. Pick a posh area and get paid more to do it. But mind your P's and Q's though! No outlay for this one, just your time. You may need to get some poo bags, some local councils give them out for free. Make sure you are walking dogs you are comfortable with and not with breeds that scare you. Also make sure you can handle any large dogs, otherwise stick to the small ones (don't forget to take your headphones with you to block out the noisy yappy ones!)

But seriously make sure you are comfortable with the ones you are walking and never take them off the lead. Losing someone's dog doesn't go down too well. As a youngster I took my neighbour's dog for a walk around the block, I let him off the lead. The dog bolted, I ran as fast as I could but couldn't catch it. I kept asking people I was passing if they had seen a Lassey dog. Yep it was that breed. Not one person saw the dog, not that I was surprised, it bolted. I got back to our house and there it was sitting outside our neighbour's house. You have no idea how relieved I was, I sure as heck won't ever be making that mistake again.

Door to Door salesperson

Okay so we have kind of covered this with Avon Calling and Betaware salesperson. If you can sell one thing door to door then you can sell anything, you use the same technique.

However, I wouldn't recommend selling raunchy underwear door to door, you might get a few funny looks, or even a few naughty suggestions for you to demonstrate the items. Best get a group of your girlfriends together for a party for that one!

Driving Instructor

I often see advertising asking for drivers to become driving instructors. You work in your own time, when you want, take holidays when you want and occasionally work weekends if you want. You can get special deals for driving cars with dual controls, I have seen brand new cars being advertised near the local test centre for less than £300 a month. Once you become qualified you will have to keep on top of your books, charge the going rate, don't try to be cheaper. You will always get custom, the world wants to drive. Always make sure you can balance the books. You will need regular car servicing, fuel, maintenance, new brake pads (learners can often ride on their brakes, well actually your breaks!) and a yearly M.O.T. All of this need to be taken into consideration as well as tax, national insurance, fully comp, etc. So charge the going rate.

This job is not suitable for those that suffer from road rage! Seriously!! You need to be a very calm person for this one!!

I remember a conversation with my driving instructor, he was telling me that a learner had complained about a colleague of theirs. Apparently (allegedly) the pupil wouldn't break, they had been told a number of times to. The instructor (allegedly) eventually after he used his dual controls, used the F word (as in 'why didn't you F***ing Break'), I guess he was trying to make a point as they weren't listening. It didn't go down too well, (allegedly) the pupil was upset and complained.

So no matter how justified (we think) we are in using the F word, don't become an instructor unless you are calmness personified. Otherwise you may find it a very short career move! Also remember you do have dual controls though, so if they don't break, then you can!

I use the word allegedly as a safe guard!!

Duck (Egg) Farmer

Duck farming, chicken farming, it's all the same thing, it's all about the eggs. Okay so ducks are a lot bigger and therefore need a bigger house. But the theory is the same. So check out Chicken Farming in this book.

There is a farmhouse near where I live that have geese going to and from their home, walking down the country lanes. It is a beautiful sight. There are also pheasant farms close by, but I don't think it's their eggs they are selling!

Ostrich eggs, now there's a thought! I am giggling at the face of your neighbour when you tell them you're going to get a couple of ostriches in your garden!! Joking aside to have any of the above, you could do with a garden big enough to house them. I don't think any garden would be big enough for ostriches though, but I may stand corrected.

E

eBay Dealer (Buying & Selling)

ebay is buying stuff and/or selling stuff (for a profit). Just remember the cost of sending the item if you are selling, the postage & packaging. You can buy pretty much anything on line these days. With this site **www.ebay.co.uk** you can bid for most things and somethings you can just buy.

Many years ago I bought my wedding dress on ebay, it cost me £16, but more than that to send it to me from China. It was still a cheap dress (it did need bringing in a bit though), it took about six weeks to get here, so be prepared for the wait and leave time for any alterations. It was worth the wait, I sold it at a boot market years later whilst having a clear out. The young lady that bought it was chuffed to bits. This dress would have cost me a fair few hundred pounds, so it was a massive saving for me.

There are also local pages on social media sites that allow you to buy and sell on them too. These are generally for items sold in a particular area, I have seen at least three different ones for my small village alone, I am sure there are more. Maybe you could even set one up in your local village or town, who knows!

Remember for those of you without internet access, use your local library if you have one in your neighbourhood. I believe you get half an hour (without charge,) a day, so make the most of it!

EBook Writer

A writer is, **a person who has written something or who writes in a particular way.**

Okay, so I have already covered this briefly earlier in the book (check out the A section, for **Amazon**). You may be reading this through one. EBooks are a way of getting your work published, you may however have to pay a small amount per sale of any book. Check out **Kindle Direct Sales** this will give you more (up to date) information on how to do it and what it will cost you, if it will cost you. Just be sure to get your work proof read by a professional and always make sure that it's printable (nothing censored, or subject to being liable).

There is a great writing magazine available on subscription, it gives you details on how to get published and there are many competitions that you can enter with money prizes available. Check out the magazines in your local newsagents or bookshop!

If you were a gardener in a previous lifetime, then you could write a book on gardening. Being retired doesn't mean doing nothing, it means enjoying what you want to do. Hobbies and activities that you couldn't find the time to do whilst working. So for all you retired professional bodies out there, what's stopping you!?! The world needs your knowledge, so start sharing it, please!

English Language Teacher

There are many ways to get to teach English to foreigners. You can do an online TEFL Course (Teaching English as a

Foreign Language). This will give you the knowledge and qualification you need. With this you can teach abroad, there are websites where you can apply for a placement to teach in many countries such as Korea, China and so on! However some of these require you to hold a degree, most of these don't specify what it is in and they just insist that you have studied at a degree level, so check it out online.

There are companies such as **www.grupovaughan.com**, this company gives you accommodation in Spain with food and board, in return for you to communicate in English to Spanish students to help them learn our language. This is volunteering and you do have to get your own flights, but you could be spending a week in Spain for just the cost of your flights. Mixing with the locals and enjoying their local cuisine. You do have to apply and they may run out of places fast, but once you request an interest they will send you the list of dates to apply for. This is done online.

Use your search engine to find out more information. Pick a country you want to go to and the search it and see what comes up. Recently a friend searched teaching English in Russia and came up with a few options, so give it a go. This is pretty much a week's holiday for the cost of a flight, but as things change over time, you will need to check it out for yourself.

Also if you have foreigners in your area who wish to speak English then you can set up evening classes to teach them, remember you don't need to speak their language just English, doing a TEFL course is great for this purpose too.

F

Flat Share

To share is, **to have a portion of something with another or others.**

Flat sharing is a great way of cutting the cost of things, such as rent, electric, water and gas. As well as your TV licence fee. Your rent and TV Licence fee won't change. Not sure how it goes with your council tax, but you will need to check it out with your local council. The idea is that you are sharing the cost with someone else.

Make sure the said someone is a person you know and get on with, once they are under the same roof there is not a lot you can do about their annoying habits or their untidiness. So make sure you vet even your closest friends as some of their habits can be hidden and until you live with them you may never see them. So just ask a few subtle questions, check out where they live and see if they keep their place clean and tidy.

If you choose to change your job for a rival company, you would do your research (wouldn't you?!?), this is no different to that. There is nothing worse than making a mistake and having to live with it (or them) for the next 6 months or so!

Ever watched the film **'Single White Female'**? (If not, then maybe you should, it is a great film, scary though!)

Flat (or house) sitting

Many people spend their time flat sitting for friends or colleagues. Families don't always pay you however, but better the devil you know! Or better the devil that knows you! Families will generally leave you with a fridge full of food and possibly some beer or wine too, whatever they know you like. Whereas if you are doing it on a professional level then you may have to supply your own food and drink.

Or they may just give you a few basics items of food stuff that they like. Although you will get paid for looking after their pad and if they want you to look after the place, it may mean that they have things inside that they need you to keep safe. Such as an extra-large TV with a paid for TV package other than your free viewing TV channels. Imagine if they had a sauna or Jacuzzi, a cinema room, a conservatory, a summer house or even a man cave. You wouldn't want to leave.

All it would cost you is the time it takes you to water the plants (if they have any), or do whatever chore they have asked you to do and are paying you to do. This isn't for everyone, although those that do this, generally love it!

You could even swap your home with a friend for one week a year (I shall explain). I have friends who live in Southampton, I live in the South West. If I fancy checking out a week somewhere else (like in Southampton) and they fancy a week where I am, then we can just do a flat swap. It's like having a free stay, the only downside is that you won't get to spend your week with your friends, (as they will be in your flat) but you could all holiday together another time of the year.

The best time to do this is in the summer when rentals are sky high. Ever seen the film 'Holiday'?! Okay so ideally you want a friend that lives in the Bahamas rather than someone who lives in your next village! But that may not happen, so I guess we just need to be grateful of what we can get.

Florist (Special Occasion Wreaths)

A florist is, **a person who sells and arranges cut flowers.**

There are many floral courses you can do and wreath making is one of them. Once you have learnt how to do it, you can use your imagination to make one out of whatever you want. For example there are Easter ones, anything can be made for seasonal wreaths. Valentines ones in the shape of a heart or with roses on them, artificial or fresh. Artificial ones can be kept safe and sold over a longer time, fresh flowers need to be sold quickly therefore can only be made last minute, which isn't practical if you are intending to make enough to sell.

Mother's day wreaths for those whom have passed away, to go on their graves. Halloween wreaths for trick or treat doors. Christmas wreaths, there are many possibilities. Also the most obvious of all, those for funeral services, you don't need to be as expensive as fresh ones (if you are using artificial flowers), but they do need to be as beautiful as them. They can be made quite personal to the person that has passed away, their favourite colour, flower or scent (sprayed with their perfume or aftershave).

If you make them well then your reputation will spread far and wide through word of mouth. So make every care to make them perfect, always listen carefully to the requests of the person ordering them and take notes if necessary. Remember this is the last gift that they can give to them, make it a memorable one for the right reason.

No one wants a bad reputation.

Foster Parent

To foster is, **to encourage the development of something, or to bring up a child that is not one's own by birth.**

There are many children in need of a good home. And there are many of us capable of giving them one. However, you will need to go through many assessments and some checks before this becomes possible. What you will need is a good home, a room for them and a lot of love and understanding. But the reward in itself is priceless, I don't mean financially. Even though you will be paid, it has always got to be about giving a child a loving home and a better start in life than the one they have had before joining your family.

Again use your search engine to find out more information on fostering. Your local council can also guide you in the right direction. I recently saw an advert on the T.V, on social media and in a local paper about wanting Foster Parents, so I can only imagine that there are many children that need a loving, caring home.

Check out the **National Fostering Agency** also **#Incredible Futures** or use your search engine.

Founder of a Charity

A founder of a charity is, **a person who has set up the said charity. They founded it.**

Many people whom start up a charity do so for personal reasons. They may have lost a loved one and feel that they need to raise money to help prevent someone else dying of the disease or illness. Or it may be a charity to help raise funds to find a cure for illnesses that incapacitate people. There are many reasons and many charities out there. So if you choose to found one, then be prepared to take an average wage, if any, as it is all about raising funds and awareness. (Some charities are there just to fund activities and help with improving people's daily lives.) This won't make you rich, but it will be so rewarding and will open different doors for you.

Your charity will need to be registered, you will need to get advice from the tax man. But above all you will need to work hard at raising money. I recently asked someone how they fund their charity (as it wasn't government funded), she said "by begging, borrowing or stealing". I doubt she stole anything, however, I understood what she meant. By any means possible.

Again, the aim is to help others, by raising funds, awareness and finding cures for whatever it is you are building your charity around. Something close to your heart is a good place to start. You do need to be persistent in what you do, don't give up the fight for funds. Networking your way to get support in raising your charities profile.

Setting up a charity is a hard slog, and you won't get where you want to overnight. Also be prepared to put in the hours (a lot of them).

G

Gaming Competitions

Gaming is, **the action or practice of playing gambling games or video games.**

There are gaming competitions that can pay you a nice and tidy sum of money, even if you are not the overall winner.

Gamebattles has awarded over $7,000,000 and have had over 60,000,000 matches played. There are many tournaments to play in and lots of competitions also. Check this out in your search engine to find out more information. If you are a keen gamer, then check it out.

Check out **fortnite world cup** there is major money to be made from this tournament. If you are into gaming then you have probably already heard of this tournament. If you haven't then check it out.

Only a few months ago I saw on the news a young lad winning a major competition. His mother continually told him off for spending too much time in his bedroom playing such games. I don't think she will be telling him off anymore!

Garage Sale

If you have enough unwanted junk that you want to sell, or just even have a clear out and you have a garage, then do a garage sale. Advertise it in your local area, with posters on trees (if you are allowed to), in your local town hall, local school, corner shop or post office. You won't have to take your stuff anywhere, just open your garage and use your drive to sell them on. There is no cost to you, just get yourself a float (cash) so as to give change. Rope a friend or two in to give you a hand, it is easy money. All you need is the contents to sell, obviously if it's a load of rubbish then don't expect to sell anything. Nobody wants a chair with only three legs, or a sewing machine that chews up all your material. So make sure you have something to sell that is worth buying!

Gardener

A gardener is, **a person who tends and cultivates a garden as a pastime or for a living.**

If you are a keen gardener and good at it, then sound out your neighbours to see if they need one. Some elderly people find it hard to keep up with the pruning and weeding. You don't have to charge a lot, just enough for your time, as time is what you should have (that may be one of the reasons you have bought this book). You could be a school leaver, a sixth former, a house wife/husband, a single parent, a retired gardener (with bags of energy), or just someone wanting to earn a little money on the side. You may want to eventually make a business out of this, so what's stopping you?!? You will need a few basic tools, if you have a garden then you probably already have them, if not, start off with some second hand ones bought from a boot market or garage sale (make sure they are good solid ones). Let your own garden (if you have one) be your show piece. Remember you do need to know what you are doing, so know your stuff!!

Grow your own (Use your Garden)

Fruit and veg are things we buy every week and although the cost may not be astronomical, it still might add up to a few pounds each week. Growing your own is a way of saving costs. Your garden doesn't take you away from your home, unlike an allotment. There are many ways to get started, books, on-line tutorials, magazines, etc. Some freebie sites give you free seeds, so do some magazines. Although I find getting your own seeds to be a better option, take them out of your shop bought tomato and put them in a piece of kitchen roll, place them in the fridge until you are just left with the seeds and not the slime. Then you can propagate them. Whatever you like, then grow it, there is no point in growing something you won't eat. If your neighbour grows tomatoes then grow something else and make a deal to share your crop. If they have nothing to share, but make great cakes, then why not ask if you can swap! Courgettes (believe it or not) taste great in cakes! This isn't about earning money, more like cutting costs by growing your own, as well as possibly sharing with your neighbour(s).

Guinness Book of Records

You cannot earn money from the **Guinness Book of records**, but you do get an official certificate of achievement for free. So if you have time on your hands and think you could do that better than the current record breaker, then give it a go. Who knows you could be in the next **Guinness Book of Records**.

This could be your claim to fame and you never know, it may open doors for you!!

As always use your search engine to find out more.

H

Hairdresser (Mobile)

A hairdresser is, **a person who cuts and styles hair as an occupation.**

Hairdressing is a profession that you do need to be qualified in, you would need to go to college a couple of days a week and work in a hairdressers as a trainee. However once qualified you can work when and where you want.

So if you are already a qualified hairdresser and want to work for yourself, then give it a go! I would print leaflets and shove them in letter boxes (if you are allowed). Use local community centres, doctor's surgeries, dentists, wherever you can put up a poster to advertise your services. Old people's homes, hospitals, anywhere where your clients cannot get out and about. We all still want to look our best, no matter how well we are, or how mobile we are.

Even on our death bed we want to look our best! Even corpses get a makeover before their final journey. However, it does take a certain person to do up the hair or make up of someone whom has passed away. I would stick with the living for now!

Hair Model

Most trainee hairdressers need models to practice on, I remember when a friend was training as one many years ago,

I let her cut my hair and I ended up with a bald patch on one side, I got her to match it up with another bald patch on the other side so it looked as though it was meant to be there. She was mortified at the time, bless her!

I did have a lucky escape though, she cut the tip of her boyfriend's ear off, luckily for him it was before she asked if he would be her model for a wet shave (with a cut throat razor). Needless to say he declined the offer! She changed her course half way through and decided to study something less harmful to people, saving any future incidents!

I don't think you will get paid but you can blag a free cut and blow dry, or a colour tint! You can even model for competitions. Once a year (I believe) you have a hairdresser competition and models are needed, if you have long hair then you could model a style for them, rather than get your hair cut by them. Once they cut it off, it's gone, so only let them do what you want them to do. Don't let them get scissor happy with your hair.

Again, blag a freebie out of it. You might be going to a friend's wedding and want to look your best, so make the agreement before deciding to be their model.

Handyman or Woman

A handyman (or woman) is, **a person which is able, or employed to do occasional domestic repairs and minor renovations.**

If you are a retired handy person, then you will always get work, the odd job here or there will give you a bit of beer money (and even a packet of crisps.) Most people would rather bung a retired person a bit of cash (one with a good reputation,) rather than end up with a cowboy who has ripped them off and left them with a big mess at the end of it. It also gets you out of the house for a couple of hours a day.

Home helper

A home help is, **a person employed, especially by a local authority, to help in another's home.**

The best way for this is to advertise as a home help, otherwise you will end up helping out your neighbours and getting nothing for your trouble. If you are helping someone whom has some sort of dementia, then try to get your fee or payment up front or get another member of the family to pay you. It will save any embarrassment later. You may never be able to convince them that they haven't paid you, so if possible go through a third person.

Don't think this is an easy ride to ripping someone off, Karma has a way of getting you back. Remember you wouldn't want someone to swindle your parents, so don't swindle someone else's! You may end up with a lot of angry family members on your case as well as the local constabulary!!

Keep your receipts (if you are doing their shopping as well), and write down your times that you have worked from and until and what work you have done in that time. Keep it all written down so you can show whomever is paying for your time. If you are working for the local authorities, then they will guide you in your work.

Home Shopper

As in home helping, keep your receipts to give to them and don't charge an arm and a leg, if you are doing your shopping at the same time, then be reasonable. A pound per shopping bag (a full one) seems fair to me, but you would need to discuss this with the person you are shopping for.

Host Family

For a few years I had used my spare room to host foreign students and I enjoyed every minute of it. Occasionally you would get a couple of unsavoury characters, but generally they are all well behaved likeable students. They varied from early teens to late fifties (these were workmen being sent over to learn English for their job) and they all had great stories to tell about where they came from and where they were heading. It was funny seeing the guy in his fifties sleeping on a bunk bed, but he loved every minute of his stay as did the nineteen year old. They became good friends oddly enough. You do need to be a sociable person, someone whom enjoys other people's company.

You get paid well for this so please don't try and skimp on the food you give them. I remember once our student told us that her friends pack lunch consisted on two slices of dried bread with a slice of cheese inside it. Nothing more was in their lunch box, I was so appalled that I went into the nearest corner shop to buy them a proper pack lunch selection. Our student would complain of stomach aches because we fed her too much, but I would rather they had too much, than not enough. However, we did have to let her help herself, that way she didn't feel bad if she couldn't eat it all.

Again, use your search engine to find the schools in your area which need host families.

Housekeeper

A housekeeper is, **a person employed to manage a household.**

Okay so being a housekeeper will remove any bills such as water, electric, gas, T.V licence, telephone and or internet bills. However, you would still have council tax to pay. You may or may not get free food also, but remember it is not your house and your home there will determine how long they want you there and how well you all get on. But if you are lonely and want a purpose in life and love to cook, clean and iron (generally love to fuss over someone) then search for jobs near you, or if you have no ties then search further afield.

This is for live-in housekeeping, but there are also housekeepers that live in their own homes and have families to go back to each night.

Vicarages have housekeepers too (or so I am led to believe), use your search engines to find out more, or get involved in your churches activities and find out as much as you can through networking. There are many professional and elderly couples that require housekeepers (as well as single professionals). You would need to show that you can do the job, housekeeping may require bookkeeping also, especially if you are doing their shopping and sorting bills etc. It depends on your level of requirement. Something you will find out when applying for any available positions.

Remember the objective is to keep a house, and to keep it well. You would have to cook, clean, wash, iron and generally keep a house a home. There are certain standards to uphold when doing this as a profession, make sure you are up to the job before applying for the position.

House sitter

We did cover a small amount of housesitting when we did dog sitting and flat sitting, they are all generally the same thing, looking after someone's home or dog while they are away. Most people hire you so that there is someone in their home while they are away on holiday or travelling for work. It is to keep the house lived in and to deter robbers from ransacking the place. Check out the F section for Flat Sitting.

I

Inventor

An inventor is, **a person who invented a particular process or device or who invents things as an occupation.**

Okay so I am not suggesting that you can earn a fortune, however I am not saying you can't. If you can invent something useful or ingenious then who knows! But if you don't try then you will never know. If you are someone with funny, whacky ideas, then maybe you should give it a go.

I remember watching the old guy in the film **Chitty Chitty Bang Bang** (If my memory serves me right) he had this invention thing going on.

Ironer

An ironer is, **a person or thing that presses the wrinkles out of clothing or other things made of fabric.**

You really have to like ironing, it's certainly not a job I would choose to do. Standing for long periods of time doesn't appeal to me. Although if you love ironing, then why not get paid to do it. You would need a car, to pick up and drop off loads, unless you expect them to drop off their washing and then pick it up. You would need to work out your costs, electric, water, car fuel, etc. Use your local corner shop or post office to advertise, also your doctors and dentist. Take into consideration how long it will take you to iron one item or twenty items. Then check out other ironing companies and then work out your fee.

Please remember to make your working area a smoke and animal free zone (best not to leave last night's curry out overnight, joking aside, it might give your ironing a bad odour and you an equally bad reputation).

J

Journalist (Freelancer)

A journalist is, **a person who writes for newspapers, magazines, or news websites or prepares news to be broadcast.**

A freelancer is, **a person who works on a self-employed basis. They can work for just one magazine or they can write for several different publications at a time. They are free to do this.**

If you have a gift of the gab or are a passionate writer, then why not be a freelance journalist. Try writing a short story or an article, you have to start from somewhere. If you have ever had to write an essay about a certain topic, of say 1,300 words, then you will know roughly what it would be like. You would also know what you would be expected to add into the content of your article.

I was recently at a leadership course and was told that if you read the first paragraph of an article, then you would have read enough, as all content will be put in that (the first) paragraph. However, if you want all the nitty gritty of information, then you would tend to read the whole article. It depends on whether or not you are interested in what you are reading, or you are just fact finding. So try it for yourself (read the first paragraph) and see what you think.

I personally love to write, but doing it as a profession, well who knows. I am sure like most things, you could possibly do a short course in Journalism, if not you could certainly do a writing course. There are many competitions you can enter too, check out writing magazines for more information.

Remember stick to the facts if you are writing a factual article, you certainly don't want to be taken to court on the grounds of slander. Your reputation as a journalist is as important as your reputation as a builder, it means the same thing, so make sure you build yourself a good one.

Junk Restorer

When I was a child my father had a catering equipment company and occasionally my siblings and I had to go with him to work to help him. He would buy second hand catering equipment such as deep fat fryers, meat slicers, to name but two, there were so any different types of equipment, but for the life of me these two have come to mind.

He would buy fryers really cheap, because they (the sellers) would tell him they didn't work, well in actual fact if they had dared to clean all the greasy fat off of them, then they would have worked perfectly. So we would occasionally do this with him and grab a piece of wire wool and get cleaning.

Once we cleaned some items up, then my father would restore them by giving them a new coat of paint (depending on if they needed it and if it warranted it). He was a bit of a restoration guy, I guess! What I am trying to say is that one man's junk was another man's fortune! If you don't mind cleaning something up and giving it a new lease of life then go for it!

There are so many restoration programmes on T.V that can inspire you and help you on your way. You will need to know what its original state was and how to get it back to that, unless you are planning on upcycling (now that's a different money earner altogether).

K

Kite Maker

I love this one, because you can do this on a rainy morning to fly on a windy afternoon. You can start with basic materials (a couple of sticks, an old pillowcase and a ball of string) and then once you have mastered it and improved on your skills you can turn your bit of fun into a profession. If you have kids that are bored then it's a great way of including them and they do tend to have a wonderful imagination. So do your own searches of the Do's & Don'ts of making a kite and then let the fun begin!

Knitter

Knitting must be one of the most therapeutic hobbies of all time. I was once told by an old manager of mine, that whilst he was in the army he was taught to knit, he was told that this would help him therapeutically, to zone out. I am not sure how true it was, however many people still use this technique as a pass time and you can earn money from what you knit. Last Easter someone knitted little animals and put a crème egg in them. They then sold them for charity for a pound each. They sold quite a few, but this was a novelty item. You may need to be more traditional to begin with.

I love blankets that are knitted and proper cardigans, jumpers, hats and scarves as well as gloves. Your outlay is a pair of knitting needles and a ball of wool. You may need a pattern to follow (you may be able to download a free one), you may even need to learn how to knit to start with. There are magazines and books that show you how to do it, step-by-step guides. Or ask a relative to teach you, if you have one who knows how to knit.

So if you have time on your hands give it a go! If you are retired and already know how to knit, then what's stopping you?!

You could even give knitting lessons to the younger generation and that will keep the tradition going on for future generations.

L

Lampshade Maker

You can find courses at your local colleges that teach you how to make Lampshades. You could even find a tutorial on-line for almost anything, so I would be surprised if you couldn't find one for lampshade making.

This is a craft and I have added this separately because I feel it can stand alone in its own right. I recently bought 2 lampshades and 3 light shades, one of these cost £80. I bought it, because I searched to find the pattern I wanted and I bought it in a large size, because to me it was a certain kind of centrepiece in my lounge, it was a statement piece if you like. I still love it and if it ever gets damaged I will either buy another one or make my own! I went on-line to buy this, used a search engine and put in a description of what I wanted and after over an hour looking for it, I found it!

If you have ever been in a vintage style shop, or a shabby chic style, full of weird and wonderful Knick knacks, then have you ever wondered where they came from?! Some shops get supplies from other shops or creative people (I have mentioned this earlier in the book). If you want to go down the avenue of making lampshades, then you need to have somewhere to sell them and it has to be somewhere where you will get a good price for them (you won't get a fair price for your efforts from a boot market).

Supply and demand is a way of supplying a vintage shop (for example), ask them what they require, agree a selling price (they can add their bit on) and then you make it and sell it to them. Some shops may pay you when they get it sold, if this is the case, then make sure you don't get a loan out to pay for the materials you will need. So keep your cost low, find your outlet to sell from or to. Keep a record of who has what, in case you are supplying more than one business with your goods. Regularly check in with them to see how your goods are selling or not as the case may be. If they have specifically asked for a certain style and you have made it to their specifications then make sure you get paid when you take it to them C.O.D (Cash On Delivery), because you have made this to order, for them! You may not be able to sell it to another person as it was made specifically for the original buyer. We all have different tastes.

Who knows, maybe I will be buying one of yours next time!

Learn a Trade

There are so many different trades out there for you to pick from and so many colleges for you to choose from to learn one. From electricians, to plasterers.

I watched a programme about buying properties abroad and doing them up and on this particular programme, there was a lady who needed a concrete layer. However she couldn't find one (for love or money), so she decided to do it herself. When the presenter of the show asked her how she managed to make up the cement she replied "I read what it said to do on the bag!" She certainly wasn't going to be beaten, however to learn a trade you need to get a qualification and you need to go to college to get it.

Although, when deciding what trade to learn make sure it is one you can make a business from and not one that every member of your family will want you to do something for them, for nothing. For example if your sister wants a new kitchen, don't do carpentry until she's had her kitchen re-furbished. If your brother needs his bathroom re-tiled, then don't become a tiler until he's had his done.

Unless however, they have a million friends that will see your work and want theirs done too, then you could make theirs your show piece, otherwise choose your trade carefully (because you can't choose your family).

Learn to Sketch

I love to sketch (not that I am very good at it), I also love to buy sketches. I once worked in a cafeteria abroad and there was a guy with his family ordering breakfast and he was sketching everything around him, this included the people, tables and chairs, it was a beautiful sketch. I asked him "how much for the drawing" he didn't know what to charge and ended up saying 20 Euros, I went over to my boss and asked him to loan me the money, of which he did. This guy carefully tore the piece of paper from his pad and signed and dated it on the back. Who knows he could be a famous artist now!

So if you can learn how to sketch, then you could earn money even in the strangest of places (like having breakfast with your family at 8 o'clock in the morning).

You will need a sketch book and a sketching pen. Courses can be done at evening class, or buy a book, visit your library, or check out the local charity shops or boot markets.

I paid 20 Euros, about 8 years ago now and it was worth every penny!

You could sketch just about anything, I have known artists sketch the outside of a bar and go inside and ask the proprietor how much will he give him for it, it doesn't always have to be a cash transaction either. A pint of larger and a hot meal could be all you need and technically it wouldn't cost them anything (financially that is, the odd pint and meal won't go a miss!).

Life Drawing Model

The only thing you need for this is a lot of balls!! Seriously sitting in a room with a lot of people staring at you can be a very nervous thing, but doing it in the altogether, well that is a different matter entirely!

Many years ago a friend of whom was studying art told me I could be a life model. I joked and said "not with my body", they said that they liked models that didn't have a perfect body! Yes, I was offended, the cheeky so and so (their body was in a far worse shape than mine, seriously!).

Anyway, where was I?! Oh yes, so if you are a bit of an exhibitionist then you could do this and I believe its pay is quite lucrative. You would need to contact your local art college to find out their availability. Or maybe you should drive further afield, so as not to be noticed by your next door neighbour of whom has decided to go to art classes in the evenings, or that friend of your mothers, you would never be able to look them in the eye again, you get my drift!

Lip Reader

Lip reading is, **a technique of understanding speech by visually interpreting the movements of the lips, face and tongue when you are unable to hear.**

Lip readers are sometimes called upon by the police to check what someone has said on video footage. You would need to be accredited to do this though, especially as your testimony could be used as evidence. So you need to be really good at what you are doing, hence getting the qualification to enable you to do the job.

Ever been away on holiday and eavesdropped on a conversation in another language, it felt pretty good eh!?! It's a bit like people watching, although lip reading is technically the same as you are eavesdropping on a conversation, but from a far. It's a bit of a spying game really, great fun though!

I recently picked up a leaflet at our local doctors surgery which offered help in learning to sign and lip read, I believe this was aimed at elderly patients of whom had a loss of their hearing (it was published for the RNID). Although it may have been aimed at parents of deaf children (or even those that have children that have Down syndrome). Regardless of whom it is aimed at, it can be for whomever wants to learn it, so check out your local surgery to find out more. Or check out the RNID, or your local college which may do courses. If you decide to study sign language, then you should be learning how to lip read at the same time, along with body language.

If you want to do this on a professional level though you will need to study for it and take the relevant exams.

Loyalty Cards

Loyalty cards are a great way of having a bit of cash for your Christmas shopping (if you want to keep it on your card for that long). I have loyalty cards for almost every shop, supermarket and eatery I can imagine.

I use my supermarket one every time I shop and generally use it for Christmas food, drink and presents shopping in December. However, if I don't need to use it then I keep it on my card. At the moment I have over £150.00 on my supermarket Loyalty Card. However, I do tend to buy a large shop of basic food stuff for our local food bank in December. It's amazing how much of the cheaper branded stuff you can get for £50.00, we try to buy six of each of the same items, that way we are helping to feed six small families.

If you are struggling financially then try to reduce your outgoings by buying the non-branded goods and try out the supermarkets own brand. Somethings, I believe taste no different to the branded items. Others can taste even better than them. If you are struggling then it is worth a try. My husband won't buy any other tea bags than our supermarkets own brand.

I have another loyalty card with £19.00 on it which I generally use for toiletries, such as shampoos and conditioners etc.

You do need to keep your cards safe, because if someone else gets their hands on them, then they can spend on them instantly. So always report your lost or stolen card right away.

There are loyalty cards for coffee shops, you generally buy so many cups of coffee and then get a free one.

You can even download apps which have your loyalty card details on them, that way you just scan your phone at the check outs. You are less likely to lose your phone than you are at losing your card.

Some supermarkets offer you a free coffee or cake in their coffee shop. I do believe loyalty cards give you money for nothing. I once had a £120.00 shop and paid nothing at the till, I just handed over my card and the points paid for it all.

M

Make Do and Mend

This is like going back to war times, when you couldn't afford to buy new, so you would have to 'make do and mend'. Patches on elbows of cardigans come to mind. Unravel an old jumper and use the wool for a scarf. You could also tart up and old cardigan by making a flower out of a piece of ribbon and attaching it to a safety pin, that way you can use it for different garments. There is so much you can do that this requires a book on its own for you to read through. Up-cycling is also another way of making do and mending. It's about revamping what you have. Use your imagination.

Make Summer Hats/Handbags

Summer hats and handbags are relatively easy to make, you can use scraps of material to make them and they don't take too long either. The more you make, the more you can sell. Don't try to be too greedy in what you sell them for, as it will take you a lot longer to sell them.

I have made summer hats and handbags out of scraps of material and sold them at boot markets (abroad) for 1 Euro each (they only cost me a few pence to make) I sold quite a few one summer, along with handmade earrings which I sold for 50 cents a pair. My fellow stall holders were not amused with me, (it paid not to be greedy) but I did make a tidy sum that year.

It's best to start making these in the winter, using summer colours and start selling them in the spring (this is usually when clothes stores will sell them). Earrings and other jewellery pieces can be sold all year round, especially a couple of months before Christmas, Valentine's day and Mother's day, etc.

The jewellery will require lots of craft stuff to make them and tools such as a pair of pliers, but most of this stuff can be bought on -line, check out **www.ebay.co.uk** I have found them extremely useful. You can sell this sort of stuff at craft fairs, rather than boot markets, you can earn more money there. I personally love the boot market side of things, you sell them much quicker there than at craft fairs. The boot market life is a refreshing way of earning money, you get up at the crack of dawn and you are done by 3 in the afternoon.

You may not earn fortunes, but you can make these from the comfort of your own home in your own time.

Make-up Model

I am not sure you will be paid for this but try and grab a free make over before a major event, such as a Wedding, Christening or even a Funeral. Let's face it we all want to look our best and it doesn't matter where we are, so even if it's at your Aunt June's (three times removed) funeral, you still want to look stunning. Or you want to bag that job in the city, or the bloke next door for that matter! You know what I mean?!

Check out your local college, or beauty school enquire if they need a model, offer your services, but make sure you negotiate either a fee or a freebie. After all time is money. Make sure it's worth your while.

Mascot Advertising/Promoting

Okay so a well-known sitcom springs to mind, laugh you may. However, as long as you keep your head on (literally), then no-one will know it's you inside and it pays, so don't knock it! Although I would do it in the winter not the summer, as it's a sweat box inside and no I haven't done this as a job personally, but if I needed the cash, then I would do it. I might just make sure it's not near where I live, as I might get taunted by the local kids. This is another one to search engine, mascots are used in sports events, as well as by companies wishing to promote their business. It's a lot of standing around, but it's a money earner. Maybe you can make your own business out of it, employ others to wear the suits, whatever you decide, don't forget to register your business, not forgetting to sort your tax and national insurance with HMRC.

Massager

A massage is, **treating the body by kneading, patting and rubbing it to stimulate circulation, relieve any built up tension and to promote suppleness.**

You need to study for this and gain your qualifications. Once qualified there is a lot of money to be made. You could work from home or (more preferable to clients) be mobile. Advertise in a posh area and then you could earn a bit extra than in a poorer area (if you want).

You could even progress to be a Sports Physio, imagine working at the Olympics or for FIFA! Olympics would be my choice, you could travel to so many countries. Common

Wealth games or marathons worldwide, the possibilities are endless. Again use your search engine and make sure you have any liability cover that you may need.

Massage Model

I believe you would do this at your own risk, as they would not yet be qualified, therefore they may cause you a bit of pain (or injury). However, I don't know many people of whom would turn down the offer of a free massage, do you?! Again, I'm not sure if this is a paying job. But done on a regular basis could do you the world of good, if done correctly. Everyone needs to practice on someone. Check out your local colleges to find out more, or search it on-line.

Metal Detector Collector

No qualification required, just the cost of the metal detector and a shoulder bag for your treasure.

Scoff you may, but seriously if they can find the remains of Richard III underneath a car park (527 years after his death), then I am sure there are still some old Medieval coins out there waiting to be dug up! However, I wouldn't suggest starting on the ground floor of a multi-storey car park though. You might find yourself in a bit of bother with your local council.

Imagine after your one thousand ring pull (from a drink can), that you eventually find your treasure. Yes it may be a slow process, but what a reward you could potentially have.

You will need to check with local authorities what items you may be able to keep and which will have to be given back to the state.

Many people look for treasures on sandy beaches, you might want to start there.

Mushroom Grower

So you wanna be a Fun Guy! Sorry I couldn't resist! Mushrooms are apparently one of the easiest vegetables to grow, yes they are the fungi family and they are quick growing, low maintenance produce. I don't think you can earn a living out of it though, however if you love mushrooms then this is for you. All you need is compost, egg boxes and a mushroom or two. They are propagated through spores and one mushroom can produce up to 16 billion spores, apparently. Anyone for a mushroom stroganoff?!!

Music Teacher

If you are a talented musician, then teaching might be your thing. It would have to be done in your home or in the home of the person you are teaching. Depending on the preference of the pupil or the parent of the pupil. Work out the going rate and then negotiate your hourly fee.

If you are not a qualified musician and cannot therefore teach, then learn an instrument and how to read music and see where that takes you first. You may prefer to be an entertainer than a teacher when you get to that stage of the process. That is a different profession entirely. But your options are open to do what you want.

Buskers earn a fair bit of money (but only the good ones, although people may pay you to go away if you sound awful, just saying!).

Mystery Shopper

I have done this my-self and it isn't so much easy money as it is more of an interesting earner. You have to remember a lot and observe everything, from what a person looks like to how the product was displayed. However, if you do as you are asked in your assignment then you will get bigger and better ones. Like spending the night in a hotel with up to £300 of expenses paid back to you, it's a great way of having a night away for nothing. You pay is low, however you get food and board for two people and all you have to do is whatever it says in your assignment notes.

For example the state of the establishment, did the receptionist ask you this or that, did the bar tender put celery in your Bloody Mary. Were you offered a side-order? Things like that.

The companies I know of are **www.marketforce.com**, **www.grassroots.com** and **www.aba.com**. I am sure there are more if you search engine it, not to be confused with the ones that get you to join a competition to win a mystery shop for a £200 voucher. Use the companies that register you and pay you from the start, even though you will need to pay for the goods, food or hotels with your own money and then claim it back. There are however some assignments that don't require you to pay anything out and they pay you a slightly higher amount than those that do require you to spend first.

You need to do everything they say otherwise you may not get paid and you won't want to be left with the £300 hotel bill.

I did tend to find my-self picking the ones that were worth having, clothes stores I would normally shop in, eateries I would dine in etc.

You will need access to a computer, a smartphone and transport. This is a very flexible way of earning money, whenever and wherever you want. You will have to register with the taxman and pay your National Insurance contributions though, as you are considered self-employed. Tax returns are quite easy these days just print off what you have earned and send it in with your returns form as proof of earnings. Also take off your expenses, fuel, also cost of a mobile phone (if you are buying one, keep your receipts), laptop, work clothes (some require you to dress smart), even a vehicle (if you need to buy one). If in doubt of what you can claim tax exemption for, then ask your local tax office, they are there to help you, believe me they have been very helpful to me in the past.

Whatever you buy for your business becomes the property of your business and not your personal property. This is worth bearing in mind if you decide to close your business. Again, get advice from your HMRC, they are well worth the phone call!

N

Nanny

A nanny is, **a person (typically a woman) who is employed to look after a child (or children) in the said child's home.**

This is something you need to be qualified for and I do believe there are schools specifically designed for this qualification. However you can obtain the certificates you need for this without attending specific schools (such as the **Royal School for Nannies**). Use your search engine to find out more.

This job you wouldn't do from your own home, you would be more likely dong it in someone else's home. The home of the child you will be a Nanny to.

You will need to search engine this and checkout which is the best one, for example which one gets you the highest pay jobs or the best countries to work in. British Nannies are wanted worldwide. You would need to check out what work visa's you may need, but first you would need to find out how long it would take to study and how much this may cost you.

There are many online courses you can do to gain the required certificates but these will not give you the hands on experience you might get from attending a school.

Once qualified you can possibly mind children in your local area, from your home, this is different from being a Nanny. However, you would need some qualifications and police checks to do this but it is another angle for you to work from home. Don't overstretch yourself though, three kids is an okay amount, anymore and you may be tearing your hair out by the end of the day.

Night Worker

Night Working isn't really something you can do from home, however it does free your days up to do whatever you need to do (remember you need to get some sleep in there somewhere during the course of the day though). You may choose to stack shelves or be a delivery driver or a postie in the sorting office, whatever you decide to do it will more than likely mean working for someone else and not for yourself.

Unless you want to be a writer, then you can work from home and in the night time, I find nights quite peaceful and therefore easier to write without distractions. There are so many people that work nights, it is up to you which profession you choose. You could be a night porter, an ambulance driver, a taxi driver, an airport worker, the list is endless.

Nurse

A nurse is, **a trained person who cares for sick people.**

Nursing is a profession of which you need to be qualified to do, unless you go in to auxiliary (you would still need to be trained). You can find a job in a caring profession, which will help you get into nursing and you can gain the relevant qualifications that way. Once qualified you can then work anywhere in the world. If you choose a certain area in nursing, such as paediatrics, you can master your profession in that area. There are so many areas in nursing, think long and hard in to which area you want to go in to. Research as much as you can and enjoy what you do, nursing is a vocation, a calling if you like. It is hard work and heart breaking, but when you get to save lives, or help bring new lives into the world, then it becomes so rewarding.

Your local college can help you get into nursing and let you know what courses are available to you. This qualification can take you round the world.

O

Online Buyer & Seller

Online buying and selling is pretty much the same as the A in the Amazon section of this book and the E in ebay section. You need to buy cheap and sell for a profit, you need to calculate postage and packaging and it needs to be something that will sell. So it's probably best not to buy 50 boxes of Christmas crackers in January, you will be holding them until November and they will take up an awful lot of space too. If you buy specialised goods, then make sure you have the contacts to sell it to, you want a quick turnover for whatever it is, and then you can concentrate on the next buy to sell.

Online Critic

A critic is, **a person of whom has an opinion of something, not necessarily favourable.**

I think many of us could be great on-line critics. You could be a foodie or a chef and then you could be a food critic. I have in my time have been a waitress working in Spain in the heat of the summer and I like to think that I was a damn good one. So whenever we are out to dinner, I find myself being a critic, either praising or not praising the waiting staff. I can't help it, I guess we make the worst customers, our standards are much higher. This is reflected in what tip I give or what I don't give. I remember being in a restaurant (in Portugal) with friends, the waiter took my friends plate away as they had finished their meal, however we hadn't and I found my-self tutting at them as they walked away with it. I couldn't help it, it was a big 'no no', but I guess they just weren't trained properly.

You can do it in other professions too, ideally write about ones you know and maybe start blogging it (see the B section in this book for Blogging). You will get followers, people like honesty, no matter how critical it is, you have to make it an honest criticism and (try to) make it a constructive one.

Online Freebies

Freebies are, **something that has been provided or given free of charge.**

There are so many on-line freebie sites to look at and get something for nothing from, you need to check them all out on a weekly basis. I cannot tell you how many things have come through my letter box over the last year alone. So the sites to look out for are **www.wowfreestuff.co.uk** and **www.magicfreebiesuk.co.uk** (I have received so much from these ones) there are many more, you will have to search engine to find them. Sometimes they require you to pay for the postage. I tend to go for the ones that don't require you to give your card details. For me free means totally free, that includes free posting. Just type in **freebies** to find more. Check out **www.moneysavingexpert.com** this is a great site which gives you advice on how to blag a freebie or two!

Online Surveys

While I was working part-time I signed up to a few survey companies to earn a bit of cash and one particular survey company paid me in first class stamps. This company was called **rmsurveys** and what you had to do was post items to an address from a post box or office near you and you would receive packages too. You had to log them on-line and you would receive the stamps and occasionally you would get special presentation packs. I used the first class stamps to send Christmas card and to enter competitions, so I was saving my-self a lot of money in a year.

You are not allowed to tell anyone (especially anyone that works for the post office that is a big no no!). The idea is that they see how long it takes to get to the destination that is why you need to keep it to yourself. You need to apply for this on-line.

There are many other on-line survey companies to use, just do a search for them. Other companies may not require you to post thing, but they will ask you loads of question and depending on the answer determines how much further they want you to go on. Some companies require you to go to group meetings or group phone calls, they pay you handsomely for this.

Check out on-line surveys and see what pop's up, most of these are done from the comfort of your own home. Always remember to cash in as soon as your payment is available, many companies cease trading and you could lose your money. However, I must say I never have. I have always been paid what I have earned.

Below are some sites you can check out for yourself:

Join.surveycompare.net
www.surveyspotter.com/online_surveys

www.ohmydosh.co.uk
www.vindale.com
www.globaltestmarket.com
www.swagbucks.com
www.onlineurveys.ac.uk
www.paidsurveysfantastic.co.uk
www.valuedopinions.co.uk
uktrustpilot.com
www.lifepointspanel.com
paidsurveys.uk.com
www.toppaidsurveys.co.uk
www.surveymoneymaker.co.uk
www.opinionworld.co.uk

There are so many more websites to checkout, just use your search engine and find out which ones suit you best. Some pay in vouchers (which is quite handy when it comes to buying Christmas presents later in the year) and others pay you in cash, you may have to wait until you have earned enough to be able to cash them in. This is not a quick fix for cash, you may have to wait a while.

Some websites you would need to be invited to join, this happens when you have joined other sites and completed certain surveys for them. You may or may not get an invite, be patient. All these surveys require a lot of time, but if you have a lot of spare time then you are onto a winner. Remember be honest with your answers they will know if you are not consistent and will then not use you. You might even get halfway through a survey when they tell you that you do not meet their criteria. So be patient and be honest with your answers. You could be rewarded with group forums which pay handsomely!

Online Testers

You are sent goods to test for companies and right a review on-line. You may get to keep the goods or pay a fraction of the price. This is a good way of getting the new up to date smart phone for two thirds of the price. Some of these companies require you to pay them for the item and then refund the money back to you when you return the goods. If you don't return the goods you lose your money, it's that simple. I have enjoyed testing many beauty creams and I have not needed to pay a penny for them, all I had to do was just write a review.

Again use your search engine to find out more.

P

Paper Round Person

It doesn't matter how old you are, as long as you are old enough to have a paper round then you can, well, have one! If you have time on your hands and need to get out of the house then give it a go. But I would recommend buying some form of trolley to put them on as your shoulder can be in agony, especially at the weekend with all of those supplements inside. Maybe you should do Monday to Friday, leave the weekend work for someone else to do.

It's a great way of getting out and about in the summer, but cold and wet in the winter, make sure you invest in waterproofs.

Most deliveries are early morning, you could be done before nine o'clock and back in bed by half past.

Party Organiser

An organiser is, **a person who arranges an activity or an event.**

I would try to find an on-line course for this one, purely because there will be so many details to think of. There is nothing more enjoyable than watching people have a good time at a party, when you are the person that has organised it. Done professionally can earn you a lot of money! You can go to your client to finalise details and you can pretty much organise things from the comfort of your own home. Your business card may not need an address, but will have your email and mobile details. Remember to register your business and your tax details as you would need to do this properly, including any professional insurances you may need.

Always take photographs and have a portfolio, keep all corresponding emails and any letters of gratitude.

Depending on venue's (size of, price of etc.), you may need certain deposits up front to pay for these, don't be afraid to ask for it. I doubt you have a spare few hundred pounds to pay for a marquee or a couple of thousand for the grounds of a stately home!

Start small, then work bigger. Try a birthday party which won't cost you a penny, take photos, rope in friends for props and see how you go from there! You could also try a christening party, or a toddles birthday bash, there are lots of places to start. Even your Nan's 90th birthday celebrations! Or organising (a surprise) for Uncle Albert's 75th birthday celebrations down the local **British Legion**!

So start small and think big, but keep your costs low until you start getting paid for the job!

Personal Trainer

A trainer is, **a person who trains either animals or people.**

There are lots of on-line courses that can go with a college course in this. Nutrition courses can help with this as well as courses that help you make people feel better about themselves, giving them support and encouragement. I am sure courses in personal training will cover these, you will need to search engine this though. Once qualified you can earn good money and even more with an outstanding reputation of getting people fit and healthy (body and mind).

Photographer (Freelancer)

There are many photography courses out there, including photo clubs for you to join. There are also competitions for you to enter (even as a novice), which you can win sophisticated photographic equipment and others where you can win cash. Some are with the wildlife organisations (I believe). This is a must to use your search engine.

There are magazines out there too, some of these cost a bit, so if you know of someone whom buys it, try and make a deal to read it after them and pay half of the price (that is if you cannot afford the full price). Or put up an advert on your local social media pages, asking if anyone has some for free, or very cheap. You could ask your newsagent if anyone has ordered the magazine, if he says yes, then ask him to give them your details (as he won't be able to give you theirs). Then when they make contact (if they do) then ask them if you can buy them from them for half the price, they can only say no! You might be pleasantly surprised though, most people are happy to save themselves money. Also check out boot markets, I have seen many photographic magazines at them in the past. If you manage to find some, then ask the stall holder if they have any more on a regular basis, if so give them your details and agree a price for them to sell them to you rather than at the market.

Freelancing comes with experience of taking good photos and knowing when and where to take them. If you know that someone famous going to attend, say Ascot for example and you are going there, then take your camera and get snapping. Make sure you have the contact details up front to send your photo's to the relevant company and make sure your price is agreed, (trust will have to be built between you and them) and there you have it, you are freelancing. Okay so it might be a bit more to it than that but you get my drift.

Be careful of how far you will go to get that picture though, no one likes a peeping Tom, so I would think twice about climbing that tree to get your best shot of someone in their own living room. You might end up breaking your leg in the process and get a ticking off from the local constabulary too!

Poker Player (on-line tournament)

Poker is, **a family of card games which involve betting.**

I love this one, it's a great one for making you feel good and it's not just for the lads. I have played with a group of men and won, maybe I had lucky cards, maybe I was just a better player, but I cannot tell you how good it felt when I won. Unfortunately I haven't played since, however never say never.

I do have friends that play in tournaments and I would like to do that one day. I recall a few years back a well know sports presenter winning £250,000.00 (I believe it was). She was quite chuffed and her co-presenter was well impressed. So all you ladies out there maybe you just need to get playing.

However, this is not to promote gambling, this is to get you to learn a skill and use it to your advantage. So think twice if you are required to pay to enter the tournament, a (small) one off entrance fee is (possibly) okay. Although having to pay a lot of money through each stage is not good. So if this is the case, it would be best to swerve this one!

As always find as much information as possible through your search engine, never go into this blind!!

Polling Station Steward

This is a great one and I have been told it pays well. Those that do this, generally do this every year and it is hard to get in on it. So my advice is to check your local council or town hall ask a few questions and then ask a few more. If you know of someone that does it then put the feelers out and let them know you would be interested. Try the next town or village too! It is a long day, but it is a great earner, apparently. There are courses you can do in becoming a steward for events, which are not too expensive (or so I am told), this might help you in your endeavour to get the job!

Premium Bonds

You can now invest in **N S & I (National Savings & Investment)** Premium Bonds from as little as £25.00, previously you had to invest a minimum of £100. For each £1 you invest you have a premium bond. The most you can invest has gone up to £50,000.00 tax free investment. I am adding this, because you have the possibility of winning money in their monthly draw. I invested and waited a month before being entered in the draw and my first entry earned me £25.00 of which I reinvested. With banks giving such low interest rates on our savings, this is a great way of saving tax free with the chance of winning in their monthly draw. Just 2 more wins of £25.00 will give me more money than I am getting from my savings account, which I have to invest into for a year. Just saying! It's worth investing just the £25.00, you never know you might just win the big amount of £1,000,000.00. Nothing ventured!!

Proof Reader

This is something that you should be able to do from the comfort of your own home. Someone writes something and you proof read it to check that it is written correctly. You may also check that the content is correct (or not it depends what they want).

You need to have some form of qualification for this, English I am sure is a must and at a high level. Try a short course in proof reading as this may be all you need! Search for courses on the web or try those I have previously mentioned such as **www.ofcourse.co.uk.**

Companies generally have their own proof readers, but with so many wannabe writers I am sure more are needed.

Q

Quick Fixes for Cash

This is for when you need cash and have none, nor do you have any about to come in. **Pawn Brokers** are there for this, however you will only get a fraction of the price of your goods (such as jewellery) unless you sell it to them, then it is gone. Pawning is a way of getting a little cash and you will have time to pay to get it back.

Ideally sell something you don't wear, something you don't want. Not your wedding ring or your mothers pearl earrings. This is because if you cannot buy it back within the said time on your ticket, then you lose it. So it's best not to pawn something of sentimental value, just in case you cannot afford to buy it back.

Please do not confuse this with loan sharking as this is NEVER a good route to go down! These are unlicensed lenders that charge extortionate interest rates and use bully boy tactics (to say the least) to get money out of you that you haven't got.

Check out the **Credit Union** in your local area to see if you qualify for a low interest loan with them. You may need to show that you have regularly saved an amount of money each month. They will give you more advice.

Boot Markets again, you will need to pay for the stall, however if you have enough stuff to sell you should be able to make the fee. Although you will need to check to see if you have to pay before you enter. If you do, then find a place that doesn't charge you. Failing that, as you will need petrol, then maybe use the Pawn Brokers first, then do the boot market and then pay the Pawn Broker back.

Garage sales are another option, which requires no money up front (although you may need some money to give as change for the goods you are selling). Or when you advertise the garage sale let the buyers know that you won't have change, no change given, correct money only. They may need to raid their piggy banks, but that is no real hardship for them.

Don't sell something you love, you will only regret it.

Sell on **Facebook**, advertise your product on your social media site. Most things are sold extremely quickly, the ones I have tried to buy are gone within a day of being advertised. Buyer collects and they generally have the correct money. You can sell anything from clothes to furniture on it. As long as it is in a good condition.

Sell your old mobile Phone, some supermarkets have a machine in their foyer that buys your old mobile phone. You put it in the machine and you get cash back for it. I think it gives you a credit note to go to customer services with (I haven't tried it my-self) and they give you the cash for it. Check it out in your local store. You can also sell mobile phones on certain social media pages too.

Citizens Advice can help to advise you of **Credit Union's** that loan you money (as previously mentioned). These organisations may help you get back on your feet.

The Citizen's Advice will help you and they are free to go to. They can also give you tickets for the local **Food Banks**. So that you will be able to eat, you will need to meet a certain criteria to get this though.

If you have any debt problems they will give you advice on what to do to resolve the problem.

They will offer you legal advice and help you with form filling. They will attend appeals with you, such as PIP (Personal Independence Payment), they can make all the difference in you winning or losing an appeal. They were invaluable to my husband when he had his appeal (they won his case and on a second occasion when they required him to be assessed, again they went to remove his payment , before it went to the appeal they told him there was no need to appeal, as they had re-thought their decision). However, they may not be able to win it for you, although they will advise you on whether they think they can. They will do their best for you. Please take into account that this is a charity and if you ever get to win you case through them, then maybe you could give then a small donation for their services. They are extremely grateful of any donations they are given, no matter how small it may be.

Gardening. If you have a lawn mower (and you know how to use it) and your neighbours grass is getting long. Then knock their door and tell them you will cut it for £10, £5 up front and £5 when it's done. They can only say "no", although if my neighbour said it to me, then my answer would be "Yes". Even though my garden is relatively small it is still hard work when overgrown.

Car washing. I would go door to door armed with a bucket in my hand, a shamy leather rag a sponge and washing up liquid. If I had to walk my whole street I would, although I would aim at the dirtiest car to begin with, they are more likely to say yes! Let them know your details so they can contact you if they need another car wash next month.

Quilt Maker

I have previously covered this earlier in the book under the craft section (I believe). There are groups of people that hold classes in the afternoon in their local village hall. There are also books on how to quilt make and college classes too. Although I feel it is relatively straight forward. You will need patches of cotton, some thread and possibly padding. Your outlay won't be much, you will need to buy pieces each week as it is an on-going thing. It will take you a while to make and it can be done in front of your TV in the comfort of your own home.

There are many boutique, vintage, shabby chic style shops that will sell these for you on a sale or return basis. You can earn more from these places than from a market stall. Check out what styles are popular before you make them as it may not be to your liking, although it might be what they can sell and quickly. You don't want them holding on to it for six months and then telling you they can't sell it. So listen to what they advise you to do, they are not trying to be difficult. They want you to do well as they make money from it too.

R

Reduce your outgoings

This is something I have done recently to identify where I spend my money. I drew a chart in my book, it was more like calendar squares and in each day I put my direct debits and standing orders in. I put them in the date that they come out of my bank. For example Lottery membership on the 8th of the month, when I had two things for the 8th, I added another box and so on. I did this in separate weeks. I had 4 weeks with extra days on each one for those that come out on the same day. It's amazing how much come out on the 10th of the month (I added five more squares for those ones). I then put a chart on the opposite page and wrote down what I had to always pay each month (permanently), thing such as Rent/Mortgage. Council Tax, Electric, Gas, Water, (I can reduce the amount I spend on my Utility Bills, by putting on an extra layer, instead of the heating, by buying a steamer to cook more veg in the same pot, instead of using all four rings on the hob and to flush the toilet less often. Your local water company will give you tips on how to cut down your usage and I am sure you gas and electric supplier may do the same). Internet Wifi (I cannot seriously live without this), Mobile phone bill (however, I can always reduce my bill by switching networks), Life Insurance (many people reduce their monthly bills by removing this one but unless you have another insurance plan available for you either through your employer or union, then you should think twice about letting this one go. Think of the person that may struggle to pay for your funeral if you pass away). I have also for me, put down my monthly subscription into a union. I know so many colleagues that always want representation but are no longer in the union. So for me this is a permanent payment. Also T.V licence unless you are exempt, you would need to check this out as recently they have made a decision to axe the free T.V licence for the over 75's. So always check what exemptions there are. Visual impaired and those that are completely blind need to check to see (no pun intended) if there are concessions for them, I believe there are for the blind, again you need to check this out as these can change from one week to the next.

In the next column I have the Temporary's, these are things such as credit cards and items bought on interest free credit. Such as my furniture, my three piece suite and my carpet (which cost a small fortune). I have just paid the last payment of my furniture off, so this will not be on next month's chart/ planner. So as long as I am paying these off, then they will only be temporary.

Now we have what I call Choose, these are things I have chosen to pay, such as lottery subscriptions, hairdressers, eating out, going to the picture, getting my nails done & having a facial. Okay so I personally don't get my nails done, nor do I go for a regular facial but you get where I am coming from. These are things I don't need to pay and if need be, I can cancel them at any time and I will then be quid's in.

Also if you have a garden with a shed then with the guttering around the shed you can catch the rainwater and have it drain into a barrel, this way you won't need to use your tap water to water your plants. This will save you money over time.

My husband and I tend to leave our shopping and other things such as eye tests and car services to do on the same day, we generally try to take the car out once a week, with the exception of going to the doctor's and my local slimming group, but these two are not too far away, the supermarkets are quite a bit further though. Although you can order food on-line to be delivered which will save you even more fuel and depending on how much you spend, you may get free delivery. I tend to get my food delivered (when I cannot be bothered to go shopping) at about 11pm, this is generally one of the cheapest delivery times and more often than not they will ring me up before 10:30 and ask if they can deliver it then. However, they never pick the products that I would pick, I have often found a bad orange in my pick before.

I love magazines, if you do too then ask your friends what magazines they buy, do a deal with them you buy it one month and they buy it the next.

You can even share your shopping (I think I will be covering that later in the book).

Re-gifting

Ever had a present given to you that you didn't want, need or didn't particularly like, then this is for you. Re-gifting will save you spending money on a present and it will stop you from having a lot of unwanted items cluttering up the place. Just remember who gave it to you, there is nothing worse than receiving it for your birthday and then giving it back to the person that bought it for you on theirs.

It's especially useful when buying a present for someone you don't particularly like, but knowing you have to get them something. We all have people like this to buy for, don't we?!!

Rent out your Belongings (Car, Caravan, Home, Garage, or Garden tools)

If you have something you don't often use then why not rent it out, for gardening and household items ask for a deposit to be paid back on return of the property.

This includes any baby equipment that people on holiday may need, such as a travel cot, pushchair, baby bath, potty, this list can be endless.

Lawn mowers and other gardening items such as strimmer's can be rented out.

For vehicles make sure you are fully comp and ask your insurers if you can hire them out. Make sure you do it properly, car hire places take your Credit Card details (for security, in case you steal or crash the vehicle). Also you would need a copy of their drivers licence etc. You need to look into it with a lot more detail and get advice, but if your vehicle is standing empty then it's worth checking out. Make sure you are completely covered and protected though and above all make sure your vehicle is in tip top condition. Get a regular service done and don't skip on any advisors given after an M.O.T. remember you are dealing with people's lives and they cannot be replaced, zero harm and safety first!

Also make sure any equipment you rent out is also in tip top condition, renting out a faulty child seat that isn't fit for purpose is not only wrong (as it is not protecting the child,) it is also illegal. I have no doubt that you don't want to be charged with manslaughter, due to the fact you neglected to check the seat for safety. It is not something any of us want on our conscience. So do it right!

Researcher

A researcher is someone who looks into (researches) something. That is what you will be doing whilst using this book. If you want to do any of the things in here to earn money then you will need to do your own research.

When I used a search engine it came up with lots of different ways to become a researcher. One said you need a degree another said you could become a junior researcher another said you can be freelance researcher.

So if someone asks you something and you don't know the answer, do you use a search engine to find it?! I do and that in itself is researching. Some publishers pay a researcher to check out the facts of a book, even a fiction novel needs to be accurate before it goes to print. There is no point writing say a thriller and saying that the Fifth Amendment is called the Tenth Amendment (for example), when it is not.

If you like looking into things then maybe this is the job for you.

Retired Worker – Odd Jobs

I believe we covered a Handyman, or women earlier in the book. Maybe a handyperson is more P.C (Politically Correct).

I also think we covered it in writing your own book based on years of experience in your dedicated profession.

This is just to say that if you are retired and your profession was fixing, building or making things, or even gardening then you can make money from doing a few odd jobs for people. Nothing too demanding, you still want to enjoy your well-earned retirement. As I previously mentioned people would prefer to pay a retired person to do a bit of work for them rather than be ripped off by a cowboy. So all you bored, retired, skilled people out there, what's stopping you!?!

Although I wouldn't recommend cleaning windows if you are not too stable on your feet, unless your sticking to the lower levels. So joking aside choose your jobs wisely, or even more so, safely. Know your limits.

Also don't undervalue yourself. If you are being asked to do a job that requires a lot of time and a great deal of your skill, then charge a fair price, after all your time is money. If you're changing a washer on a tap then you are not going to be asking for fifty quid. But if you've had to strip down the washing machine to fix it and put it back together again, then you will be asking for a larger amount. So price yourself wisely, but also fairly!

S

School Runner

Many parents doing the school run are working parents. So if you have free time on your hands, are police checked, are fully insured to take passengers in your car, have regular services of your car and have dealt with any advisors given in your M.O.T then why not be a school runner. Obviously you need to do a bit more research to check that I haven't missed anything out and you need to have a big enough vehicle for the amount of children you need to run to school. So unless you have a people carrier or a mini bus, then stick to three children in the back and depending on age, weight and height (you need to check this out too) you may be able to put one in the front. So a maximum of four passengers. A clean licence is advisable.

Seasonal Seller

This is where you buy seasonal stock to sell. You would need to buy Christmas stock in the autumn to give yourself enough time to sell it. Halloween stock in the summer. Summer stock at Easter and Easter stock in February as well as Valentines stock in January. There would be no point in buying Christmas stock in December as you won't be giving yourself enough time to sell it and most people would have bought their decorations already.

As for presents some people buy them in the January sales and keep them tucked away for the next eleven months (that includes me).

Whatever job lot you go for, make sure they aren't dodgy! It's no fun buying Christmas tree lights that keep flickering on and off (if there not meant to). Or selling an inflatable Santa that just keeps on deflating!! So sell the best you can get (make sure you can make a profit though), don't overcharge them. Otherwise you could be holding on to them until the following Christmas. Small profit quick (and high) turnover works well.

Sell your designer gear for less

Selling on social media is a big thing at the moment, you post your item with a description and the price and wait for someone to message you their interest. I work on the basis of asking for a little more than I want, that way if I get offered a bit less, then that's okay. Always be honest about the condition, the buyer won't be pleased if they have driven a distance to buy it and it turns out to very poor quality or to be nothing like its description.

Share your Shopping (with a Friend)

Many times I have shared a bag of carrots with my best friend but why stop there? Compare shopping lists, see what you both need or want and split the cost. There are some things that if you buy in smaller packets cost more money so that is when we need to 'share our shopping'. For example last week I bought 3 items of meat for £10, which in itself is a good deal. However, there were three different meats you could buy, chicken breast, a steak and pork chops. These are what I bought, for me the pork chops were the best deal. So in the packet of pork were 8 thick chops, if I had bought the chops (3 lots of them) then I would have had 24 to share with a friend, 12 each for £5 not a bad deal. Although if I had 12 friends we could have 2 chops each for less than 84p per person. It works out the same price per chop, it just means you don't have to buy so many on your own. Okay so I doubt you are going to rope in 12 friends to do this, I may stand corrected! But this is just to demonstrate the difference to you!

You can share a packet of toilet rolls or washing tablets, dishwasher tablets (if you are lucky enough to own one). Bin bags, kitchen rolls even pet food, split your tins of tomatoes or baked beans. If you can easily divide it, then why not share it?!

I mentioned sharing magazines earlier as a way of saving you money. After all, don't you sometimes borrow an outfit for the night and vice versa?

Another way is also to try and buy magazines at a boot market, you can even (as I mentioned in the P section for Photography) ask the stall holder if they will get any more, give them your phone number so they can contact you so you get them before they go to the market.

At the moment there is a massive campaign to end Period Poverty. To try to get companies to foot the bill for sanitary products and to get our government to also. With that in mind if you buy the bigger packets of products and split them with a friend, it may save you money. Just until we get them supplied to us for free by government! It would be no good sharing a standard packet but the larger packets would be a benefit to us to share!

Shorthand writer/Secretary/Note taker

There are many books to teach us shorthand and courses too. I feel that this is something that should have been taught in schools. However, as it's not, try your local Secretarial College which should cover all of this combined. It may cost you some money, but it is a skill these days that can pay a tidy sum. You can get on-line courses which will be considerably cheaper than a top secretarial school, although I find being taught in a classroom is a better way of learning for me. That is just my personal preference, we all have different learning techniques. Whichever way you decide, make sure it's the best way for you!

Short Story Writer

There are writing magazines that offer courses available to help you to learn how to write short stories (or at least advertise classes in short stories). These magazines also have competitions and they also advertise other competitions inside the magazine for other organisations.

Go to your local supermarket or shops to check out the magazines available for you to buy. I have found **Writing Magazine** very informative with lots of competitions inside, some are tucked away, but if you are going to read it all the way through then circle them as you go, I did just that. There are other magazines to check out so find your nearest retailer in magazines to check it out. They are well worth the cost, some of the competitions inside offer £250 prize money. You can order a magazine from your local newspaper shop, this will save you time not going into town. Or you could subscribe them to be delivered to your door, you generally get a reduced price for this!

Song writer

There are books for **Dummies** (no offense intended), these are designed to teach us something that we know nothing about. There is even one for Song writing. Most artists have songs written for them, I once read that Elvis Presley never wrote his own songs, I don't know how true that is. Although it is hard to imagine that he hadn't written any of them (yes I am a fan of his!).

I have also read that songwriters can earn more money than the artist that sings their song. So if Elvis didn't write his music, yet earned such a lot of money (I know a massive understatement) then how much money did the writer earn?! That is if what I read was true! Never the less, if you have a gift for writing, song writing, then maybe this is the way to go about it!

Not much of an outlay for this one really, just a pen and paper and some imagination.

Study (to be anything you want to be)

There are so many things that we can study at from the comfort of our own home. You will just need to decide on what you want to do! There are so many learning courses, tutorials to choose from. I have listed a few throughout this book. But you really need to search what you want to study and all the information you need will be at your fingertips. To study you will need a laptop (or desk top computer) and internet access.

Surveys for Stamps

I had covered this in the S section (for Surveys). It is a great way of getting stamps. It's easy to do, just stick to the rules and you'll be fine.

T

Teach English as a Foreign Language

We have covered this in English Language Teacher. TEFL as it is known can open so many doors for you to work abroad, if you have a degree in any subject (they just want to know that you have studied at that level), you can work in Korea, China, Thailand and many other countries.

There are many websites that offer you jobs to apply for abroad. You can also get help from your TEFL tutor once you have qualified. It is an online course and I personally found it very interesting. Once you have completed all the units you will be sent a certificate and then you can check out where you want to go.

Teaching English in Spain

I have also previously covered this in English Language teacher. For more information contact **www.grupovaughan.com** to apply for voluntary teaching in Spain. Your food and board will be covered. You will just need to pay for your flight. Check out the site. You will be glad you did. You don't need to be an English teacher, you just need to be English to communicate with Spanish people in English. You will be able to enjoy your evenings and even enjoy them with the Vaughan Group and taste the typical Spanish cuisine. What's not to love about this?!

I have applied for this before unsuccessfully, as I could only fit in one of the weeks and I wanted to stay in the one in Madrid at the time (it looked the nicest, very scenic). However, if you are not tied to anything and can apply to all of them, then I am sure you will get a place and who knows they might ask you back or ask you to stay! Now there's a thought!

Teach yourself from Home

There are so many teach yourself books and so much for you to learn. You just need to know what it is you want to learn then find the appropriate book. You can use tutorials on-line or on-line courses to help you. But teaching yourself generally means just that. Check out your search engines to find what you are looking for. If you have time on your hands then you could literally teach yourself anything, from knitting a scarf to how to strip and rebuild a car engine!

Telephone Sales Person

Cold calling, I'm not keen on these type of calls, I don't trust what I am being told, nor do I have the time or the inclination to listen to what they are trying to tell or sell me, even if it is beneficial to me. But if you love to talk and don't get disheartened with customers like my-self, then give it a go. Some people (I believe) can work from home.

Sometimes when we ring up our telecommunications provider you end up ringing a call centre. These people are there to help you, this is different from one trying to sell you something.

There are also people that talk to you about sex over the phone, this is a different thing entirely. I believe you call them, not the other way around. Although you are talking on a phone and being paid to do it. I think you need to talk dirty though, not sure I could do it. I would be in fits of giggles but if you have the voice and confidence then why not give it ago?! I don't think it's illegal, is it? If it is then disregard this, forget you ever read it! If you can!

Touch Typist

The quick brown fox jumps over the lazy dog.

This sentence has all of the letters of the alphabet in it. (I have checked it for my-self!) If you practice this, then you will learn where all of the letters are. Practice it even more and you could be on your way to be a touch typist. Touch typing is when you do not look at your keyboard you will just need to look at your screen, or if you are typing from another document then you will be looking at that. If you are typing from a Dictaphone then you will be looking at the screen and listening at the same time. Alternatively, you can go to a secretarial college. Check out what is available in your area.

Translator

A translator is, **a person who translates from one language into another.**

You would need to be qualified for this and you would need to produce the qualification for it. Even if your mothers tongue is of the language you are being asked to translate into English. Police use translators and imagine that the translator got it wrong and wasn't fully qualified, then that drug dealer around the corner got off on a technicality. Hypothetically, obviously! So when you stand up in court (do translators stand up in court?) you can testify with confidence that you know what you're saying and the Crown Prosecution Services can feel confident of that too!

I do recall that when you got to A 'Level standard you had to spend a year in the country who's language you are learning. I don't know if much has changed since then, but you will need to check it all out. I still believe you need a degree to translate though, but check it out, I could stand corrected.

Tutoring

A tutor is, **a person who provides assistance or tutelage to one or more people on certain subject area or skills.**

If you search how to be a tutor then you will get some guidance on this. I believe most patient people can tutor a child or even an adult. Whomever you tutor, you will need to have a curriculum and or a learning plan to go by. The local education authority can help you with that. If you are a qualified maths teacher, or mathematician, (for example) and you are giving children extra tuition their parents can tell you where their weaknesses and strengths are that way you will know where to begin. You will need the usual police checks as parents need to know their children are in safe hands. Even if you are teaching them in their own home and in front of their parents.

Good tutors earn a good wage and word of mouth will get you in undated with work.

U

Upholsterer

An upholsterer is, **a person who upholsters furniture. To provide furniture with a soft, padded covering.**

There are short courses available for this to do in colleges. (On-line tutorials are available also.) Check out your local college for more information on when and how much the course is and what you will need. Like a chair or foot stall to work on. I have friends who will not give up their old solid, comfortable sofa even though it is on its last legs. That is where an upholsterer would come in handy. Sofa's these days are not made to last, mine is a year old and it's become so uncomfortable that I choose to stay in my nice little armchair. So I can see where they are coming from.

Making a business out of this is not going to be easy as you will need a workshop, tools (unless you already have them) and your materials and fabric which will cost you. You are not likely to be paid until you have it finished. Some companies will asked to be invoiced and will pay at the end of the month. So unless you have a great business plan for your bank manager, you are going to need savings. Ideally you would have a full time job and start saving before you decide to do a course. Working another job and doing your upholstery for a living won't work. You would need to do it solely otherwise you will be tired and it will show in your work. Which will generate a bad reputation and nobody wants that.

Use your Know How (Sell vases to Florists, or ice to Eskimos)

Auctions are a great place to find items to sell on, I have bought a box full of vases and taken out a couple and sold some of them, I even went into the florist to sell them. I only paid £4 for the box (that's the bonus of no one else wanting to bid for them). I kept the crystal one for myself and those I didn't sell or want, I gave to the charity shop in town.

My point is if you know someone would buy something from you then you know you can sell it on. It's the gift of selling but also if you know they sell items like that then you have a chance of them buying it from you. Bicycles at auctions is another one. As long as no one is bidding against you, then you can buy them relatively cheap. My one cost me £8, it was a bargain really. If you know of a second hand bicycle seller then you could sell it to them for more than that I am sure. Brand new bikes cost up to £300 (I believe, the standard ones). So if you can sell yours for £50 and it only cost you £20 then that is a nice profit. It might be worth doing a bit of research on this. Check out your second hand buyer find out how much on average they will pay for a bike and then you can work out your maximum to bid for.

If I was getting £50, then I don't want to pay more than £25 and that's to sell on without doing any work to it at all. I would be going straight from the auction to the buyer within the hour. This is all very much like dealing, know where to sell it on to and you are half way there already.

V

Value your Opinion on Forums

You need to use your search engine for this, we covered surveys earlier in the book. This is one step further, it's asking for your opinion and they are willing to pay for it. What more could you ask for. You may be asked to go to group chat to give your opinion on something, you are paid well for this one. Again if you have time on your hands then it is worth doing. You may even be asked to give your opinion over the phone. This is easy money, you do however need to be honest. If your answers contradict each other then you won't be asked to do it again. Nor will you be asked if they realise you are trying to give them answers you think they want, which means you are not giving your true opinion. I have done surveys that try to catch you out, so believe me, these people know their stuff.

Volunteer Services to get noticed

To volunteer is, **a person who freely offers to take part in an enterprise or undertake a task.**

If you want to get into a certain line of work but cannot get an interview for love nor money. Then try to get in the back door by doing voluntary work for them, get yourself noticed and show willing. Let them see you are an asset and that you have a skill in what you are doing. Keep your ear to the ground and do a bit of networking while you are there, always be polite and well mannered. When you hear of a position going, get in there and work for it. They would have seen how you work and know exactly what they are getting for their money. So make sure they see the dynamic get up and go type of person you are.

Not all companies have volunteers, however I would certainly take on a volunteer if I was getting a worker without paying for the privilege.

If they still don't want a volunteer then try to offer I weeks work for nothing and then let them know how much of an asset you are. Increase sales, increase productivity, whatever the business is, make it shine in that week. Then at the end of the week give them your details again. If they don't get a hold of you on the Monday (I am assuming you have just worked the Monday to Friday), then go back on the Tuesday. If they say they cannot afford you, remind them that they cannot afford not to have you. Agree a fee for the first month, let them check the increase for that month (you need to make sure it isn't a decrease as that's not going to help you). When they've worked that out, sit down and negotiate. They may want you to continually increase sales, as long as they pay you for it, agree to it. Remember you are doing a great job, now you need to be paid for it.

I am not saying all this would work, it depends on a lot of things. What type of job you are going for and what sector it is in?! Let me explain, if I wanted a job in the local pub, I could do a trial and increase sales in drinks and food and have the locals eating out of my hand. I can sell whatever the cook wants me to promote first, steak, fish and chips, whatever it is I can do it. I can sell ice to Eskimos. I do the trial, then go, the locals don't eat or drink so much, food gets wasted, sales are down. I go back and agree a payment for the first month (all be it a little lower than I would like). After the month we sit down go through sales and work out achievable targets to which I would agree, we would discuss the menu (what does and doesn't sell). Then we negociate my pay, I either get it or I go, simple as. I have proved my worth (invaluable), I have done everything I have set out to do. I'm not asking for fortunes, just the going rate.

If you are as confident as me in what you can achieve then give it a go. Some businesses don't know they need you until you show them what you can do. More importantly what you can do for their business.

However, if you want to land that job in Pharmaceuticals then you may have to be top of the class at University. There is only so much I can do to help you!

Fundraising is a great one to volunteer in, if you like that kind of thing. It is a hard slog though, but you can become invaluable to them if you are good at it.

Some local garden centres have volunteers too. Fancy being a barista? Then ask your local coffee shop if they need help on a Saturday. Once someone says 'yes' you are halfway there, the rest is up to you.

I have worked for companies that took on work experience youngsters after they finished their schooling. Work experience is free labour, it shows the company how you work whilst giving you the experience of working. This really isn't much different to that in volunteering. Or giving them your services free for a week, it's pretty much the same thing.

I am not saying you will get the job or get to volunteer but let's face it if you have tried every other avenue then give it a go. You have nothing to lose if it is the job you want!

W

Wedding Planner

I do believe I have covered this in party organisers, this is just a step up really. There are on-line courses for this and this would be invaluable to you. If you are a good organiser and have a stylish approach then give it a go.

Always listen to your clients, it is their day to shine. You are just there to make it happen and that is exactly what you have to do. If they are overwhelmed with happiness then that will make you elated, it means you have delivered exactly what they wanted. Everyone will be talking about you for the right reasons and that will generate more business for you.

They may be asking you for the impossible at times, you will need to make it happen! Never look as though you are out of your depth, remember this is what you have studied for, you are quite capable of doing it.

Once you find out what they want, find out the cost (of everything you will need, even toothpicks on the tables). Then add on your fee or percentage, remember weddings are (for the couple) years in the planning. You need to work it all out, and have everything in place, then 48 hours before the wedding you will be full on with the preparations (or even 72 hours before hand, depending). What I am trying to say is you won't be getting much time to rest during the final hours. Even the following hours after the celebrations as you will need to send back anything you have hired. Pack everything away in their packaging and any final details you will need to do.

Don't forget to keep a portfolio, no one will be taking your word for it and yes I know you have to start somewhere, so maybe start with Party Organising.

Don't forget to sort out your tax and national insurance and register your business at Companies House. If you don't then don't be surprised if you don't get any business. Because that will be the first place I will look to check to see if you are a legit business.

Window Cleaner

This is a job that keeps you out and about (not one you can do from home). You will need a good set of ladders, a bucket, a sponge, squidgy and a shamy leather to do the job. You will need transport and I don't mean public (I am picturing a person trying to get on a bus with an eight foot ladder). A van or estate car with a roof rack. Set yourself a fee that doesn't require you to carry too much change, £5, £10, depending on how many windows, how difficult it is or how long it takes. You will also need a bum bag (or something equivalent) to carry your money in and a receipt book. Businesses will require a V.A.T receipt to claim the tax back. Don't forget to register at Companies House and sort your tax and national insurance out.

This job is not for anyone suffering from vertigo or someone afraid of heights!

Win Prizes via Freepost (or for the cost of a stamp)

There are so many competitions that you can enter by writing to them via freepost, so they won't cost you anything. If you check on the TV when the competitions come up, you are told a phone fee and you are also told you can send it to wherever, some you can also do free on-line. Some require a price of a stamp (when I did the post office surveys I used some of my stamps for this).

I have I must confess NEVER won anything, although I have had a colleague that would win prizes through competitions, she would enter as many as she could, from magazines mostly. Magazines cost money, so unless you can get to check them out in your local doctors, dentist or hairdressers then you might want to stick to what's available to you for free.

Sharing magazines is also a way of entering competitions, as long as you don't have to fill out and send the coupon in, as there will only be one in there. Although you could possibly agree to share the prize as long as it isn't something that would be impossible to share or cut down the middle. Two halves of a kitchen (half in your house and half in theirs) doesn't really go, does it?! This is something you would need to discuss in advance with your bestie!

W.I. (Women's Institute) Get into Competitions

Most villages (like mine) have a Women's Institute Meeting once a fortnight. **www.thewi.org.uk** is the site you need to go to find out their diary dates, you can also find a meeting near you, or learn how to create your own meeting. So check out the site, apparently it is no longer just about 'Jam and Jerusalem'.

This is a women's group, however they do have fetes where you can win competitions and I am not sure they are solely for women. Check out the web site to find out more.

For all you women out there though, young and old, this is a great way of getting out of the house and mixing with other women in your area. You can compare experiences and lots of other things. This one is more about your well-being and it is only once a fortnight. You may meet your new best friend there!?!

X

Xbox Games seller

If you are a gamer then you will know exactly what I mean when I say that the first day or early release day for games is crucial to a gamer. They pre-order or they just queue until the doors open for them to get that game straight away! They don't wait til pay day, they have already been waiting for that release date for the last month or so!

However, if you need cash then selling your old games can earn you a nice amount and today selling on a social forum is your best bet. Children don't have the same amount of cash as adults so if they can buy them later and cheaper than the original price then they will. I am not sure on the average price of a new game, although I am sure we bought our grandson one last Christmas for almost £40, so if you sell them for £20 a few months down the line then you're getting 50% cash back. Just saying! Selling two old ones gets you a new one!

Y

#YBF You've Been Framed

This is a show that pays you £250 for every video of yours that is shown on their programme. You can download them at **itv.com/framed**, however you video needs to be funny, if it isn't then I doubt it will be shown. It also has to be natural and not a staged performance. So if you haven't seen the programme before, check it out on a Saturday early evening. You can even go to **itvplayer** to see past episodes.

So if you have an animal that does funny tricks, or a clumsy friend or have just videoed something at the right time and the right place, then give it a go. Remember it must be funny. I believe that someone seriously hurting themselves doesn't count as funny. Nor would a near death experience. So just stick to the funnies.

Yoga Teacher

Again check out your local college for classes and your search engines to find out about on-line courses. You will need a classroom or a room in a Gym for you to do your class in. Gym's normally have mats for you to use. If you are using a village or school hall then you may need to buy your own mats or get your pupils to bring their own. Other than the cost of the course, the mats and hiring out the room, there is not much more to lay out.

You still need to register your tax and national insurance though, so calculate your costs accordingly and keep any receipts you have, such as petrol, mats etc.

If you did two classes a day, then you could be on a little earner. Check out other village halls to see if they have classes or not. Preferably in the next villages surrounding yours.

If you class is big enough for 20 people and each person pays £5 for the class (which generally last an hour), you are looking at £100 per class. Two classes a day five days a week could earn you £1,000 before your stoppages. You could be looking at £600 (more or less) a week. You need to check out your outgoings and have a chat to the taxman to get a better idea of what you could be taking home.

You also need to check out any insurances you may need to take out (such as public liability), you just need to do your homework. Personally if I could take home £2,000 a month for two hours work a day then I would be laughing all the way to the bank.

This is a great one for those that are working around children or those that don't have much free time. You could be a part-time student, this would certainly help with any fees you may need to pay. You can also check out your local rest homes and see if you can make a deal to teach yoga there. There is a lot of opportunity here to earn money without exhausting yourself in the process.

YouTuber

If you can download something on YouTube depending on how many hits you have depends on what you can earn, or so I am lead to believe. Go to your search engine and type in 'How to make money on YouTube'. This will give you a video to watch. Then the rest is up to you!

Z

A Zumba teacher, yoga teacher (go to the Y section to find out more), even a fitness teacher, they are all basically the same. Get your course sorted and earn your certificate. Then find a hall or classroom and get going. Don't forget to get your national insurance and tax sorted, as well as any liability insurance that you may need.

This is more energetic than yoga, but it is great fun and a good form of exercise. Check out which will suit you best, this or yoga, or maybe you fancy Salsa, or even line dancing, who knows? The choice is yours.

I hope you have found this book useful and that it has given you the confidence to try at least one of these listed to either help you improve your finances, re-educate yourself or earn an income from the comfort of your own home.

I thank **Bing** search engines for giving me the definitions I have listed and included in this book.

For me my favourite one was to win in a chess tournament, let's face it we play to win. So my new challenge is to learn to play chess and to play it well!

Whatever you choose to do, I wish you well in your endeavour!

A to Z Index